THE *Healing* DESERT

THE Healing DESERT

IN THE SANDS OF TIME

MONA HADEED

authorHOUSE®

AuthorHouse™ LLC
1663 Liberty Drive
Bloomington, IN 47403
www.authorhouse.com
Phone: 1-800-839-8640

Published by AuthorHouse   11/19/2013

ISBN: 978-1-4918-2935-6 (sc)
ISBN: 978-1-4918-2934-9 (hc)
ISBN: 978-1-4918-2936-3 (e)

Library of Congress Control Number: 2013919080

Table of Contents

Dedication

This book is dedicated to *the Year of Faith*.

Pope Benedict XVI proclaimed the Year of Faith, beginning October 11, 2012, and concluding on November 24, 2013, the Feast of Christ the King.

The start of this Year of Faith coincided with the anniversaries of two great events in the life of the church: the fiftieth anniversary of the opening of the Second Vatican Council, and the twentieth anniversary of the publication of the Catechism of the Catholic Church. I find it fitting that I complete my autobiography in 2013, a year that holds so much significance to my Catholic faith.

As we contemplate the meaning of this, we can all identify the many ways in which we have journeyed in our lives, the road of faith, and ask ourselves how we ever survived, if not for faith and the presence of God leading and guiding us.

We walk many a narrow, dark, and winding road; thankfully, if not for the faith passed onto us, we may have been swallowed up by the fears and anxieties that overwhelm us.

I pray that my journey would bring hope and courage to those who feel that in darkness, there can be no light.

As Mother Teresa once said:

> "I always say
> I am a pencil in God's hands.
> He does the thinking.
> He does the writing.
> He does everything and sometimes it is really hard, because it's
> a broken pencil and he has to sharpen a little more.
>
> "Be a little instrument in His hands so that He can use you
> Anytime, anywhere.
> We only have to say
> "YES"
> To God." [1]

---

[1] Mother Teresa, *The Joy in Loving: A Guide to Daily Living*. New York: Penguin Compass, 2000.

"Now faith is the assurance of things hoped for, the conviction of things not seen" (Hebrews 11:1).

"Faith is: standing firm in what one hopes, being convinced of what one does not see. Faith draws the future into the present, so that it is no longer simply a 'not yet.'

"Knowing how to wait, while patiently enduring trials, and it is necessary for the believer to be able to receive what is promised" (Pope Benedict XVI Encyclical Letter: *Spe Salvi*—In Hope We Were Saved).

Hebrews 10:36 says, "For you have need of endurance, so that you may do the will of God and receive what is promised."

Faith is the divine assurance that when we lift up our cup of sorrow, it will become our cup of blessings.

In Thanksgiving

I would like to give thanks to God, who has saved me from the perils of death, for new life and joy in the spirit, to love and serve Him in this world and the next.

In my final decision to write this book, I realised that this year, I am celebrating my sixtieth birthday and my thirtieth year of being free from cancer. How fitting it is to glorify God for the great things He has done for me! **"And Mary said, 'My soul magnifies the Lord, and my spirit rejoices in God my Saviour, for He has regarded the low estate of his handmaiden. For behold, henceforth all generations will call me blessed; for He who is mighty has done great things for me, and holy is His name." (Luke 1:46-49).**

My gratitude for the return of my life and the restoration of my good health has given me the strength to continue my journey; nothing was too much nor too hard for my God to handle on my behalf. Thank you, thank you, the wind beneath my wings.

Foreword

Many of us can say that life has treated us unfairly at times, and I'm certain that we each have a story to tell about the joys, trials, hardships, and hurts in our lives. What causes someone to publish a book about their life, or keep it hidden in their hearts, I cannot say, and only the Lord knows. But if inspired pen is put to paper, with much uncertainty and fear, *it becomes a reality*.

My journey with the Lord has always been one of testing and trials. Complete faith and trust in the Lord seemed impossible and supernatural. Over a span of thirty years, different incidents have helped to shape my spiritual journey, bringing me to my resting place.

Father Henri Nouwen, one of my favourite writers, once said:

"Your spiritual journey is as unique as mine. It has its own unique beauty and unique boundaries."[2]

Unknown to me, God was calling me to embrace many difficult situations, which would cause me to draw on all that He had taught me, throughout the years of my spiritual growth.

As you read further into my story, you will notice that my faith became stronger, and through every difficult situation, I believed, witnessed, and proclaimed that my God never fails me.

I moved from believing to trusting.

I learnt the meaning of abandonment and divine providence and how one's soul can achieve the highest degree of sanctity, by simply accepting the sufferings that the Lord has ordained for them.

The years of my spiritual growth led me to understand that as we grow closer to God in our journey, the desire to please and love Him with our whole hearts surmounts all, and challenges us to accept whatever comes our way with love and fortitude. As a result of this, we are united in spirit with God, whom we love.

"I must not fix my attention on things, people, circumstance, or events. Those are only passing elements in the drama of my life. In a certain sense, they are really illusions, not realities, and therefore make a poor foundation

---

2   Henri J.M. Nouwen, *Here and Now: Living in the Spirit.* New York: Crossroad Publishing Company, 1994.

for faith. Only God is my 'Constant', my abiding One, as the Bible stresses, and all else is for a 'Season.'"[3]

In 1986, on my pilgrimage to Medjugorje, I was struggling with accepting the will of God for my spiritual life. At the pilgrimage, I shared my fears and uncertainties with a priest, who suggested that I recite the following prayer on a daily basis:

> "Father,
> I abandon myself into your hands;
> do with me what you will.
> Whatever you may do, I thank you:
> I am ready for all, I accept all.
>
> Let only your will be done in me,
> and in all your creatures—
> I wish no more than this, O Lord.
>
> Into your hands I commend my soul:
> I offer it to you with all the love of my heart,
> for I love you, Lord, and so need to give myself,
> to surrender myself into your hands without reserve,
> and with boundless confidence,
> for you are my Father."[4]

Charles de Foucauld
The Desert Father

In discovering this prayer, I came to realise that happiness lies in the daily acceptance of the will of God, while striving to endure, with joy, all that comes our way. I repeated this prayer each day, until I reached full surrender to all of the doubts and anxieties that I experienced on my journey. *I had to trust Him.* It was hard and painful, but God's grace carried me as I entered deeper and deeper into the will of God for my life.

I share my story with you in order that you may understand that God allows us to experience our trials to build our strength and soar on eagles' wings, knowing that God carries us with His footprints in the sand.

---

3   Glyn Evans, *God's Perfect Plan for Us.*

4   Charles De Foucauld, Robert Ellsberg, *Charles De Foucauld: Writings.* Maryknoll, NY: Orbis Books, 1999

"It is no easy task to live with all the sorrows that we bear. Often, we are hindered by our wounded past, until we call on the name of Jesus at last.

"His love is forever, and His peace endures. If we stay here in His name we'll feel the cure. He hears us crying our silent tears, so we stay as close as fear will let Him hear.

"Even as we bleed while we dress another's wounds, we are left feeling lonely, feeling hollow and used, until we reach for what is true."

Author unknown

Acknowledgements

Ten lepers were healed by our Lord, but only one came back to give him thanks. To the leper who came back to give thanks, Jesus said, **"Rise and go your way; your faith has made you well"** (Luke 17:19).

In the joy of all of our healing, we tend to forget the ones who have been instrumental in making it all happen. I apologise if I have forgotten to mention anyone; I pray God's blessings upon you and your families.

To Rosemary Hadeed, with whom I shared the secret of my decision to finally take the plunge and publish my book, she listened to me and encouraged me. May God bless you and your family and grant you your heart's desires.

Thank you, Sister.

I would like to give my heartfelt gratitude to Anthony Hadeed, who came to my rescue each time my computer failed me. I could not have finished this book as quickly as I did, if it were not for his computer advice and expertise. He always came when I called; I pray that God will reward him graciously and may the "joy of the Lord be his strength."

Thank you, Brother.

To all those whom the Lord placed in my life over the years, you have made up part of the story of my faith and endurance. Without you, this book would not have had the stories it did. Your "yes" to the call gave birth to the stories I had to tell, unknown to us that one day, they would come together to form a book. God chose all of you to share a part of this faith journey with me. A special thank you to my spiritual friends, who I know have carried me all the way in prayer. Their promises to call my name before the presence of the Almighty have produced great fruit. May God reward you abundantly and protect you as He did for me and my family.

Thank you, Family.

Mona Hadeed

Finally, to Megan, my local editor: it was a spiritual experience to work with you, and as with a little child, it was heart-warming to see you blossom with the confidence needed to share your editing skills with me. Thanks for encouraging me to be more open in my experiences so that my readers can capture the real truth of my story. You urged me on when I was not sure, and I raised you up when you were down. Good luck in your future.

Thank you, Megan.

Sentiments

The Healing Desert: In the Sands of Time centres on a journey of faith. It emerges from Mona Hadeed's handwritten entries of a simple journal, and it spans many years. She recorded the faith-building events of her life, guided by a sense that they would not always remain private, though she did not know how or when they would be revealed.

Mona paused many times during her life experiences to consider different people who would be best suited to review her writings and assist in formulating them into a book, but she hesitated, holding strong to the conviction that the person should be unknown to her so that he or she could remain objective and unbiased.

Following the death of her husband, and a pilgrimage which prompted her to focus on the completion of her journal, she was led one night with great urgency to share her journal with a brother in Christ. She asked him to read it and to pray for guidance, as she did not know how to proceed. After doing so, they prayed together, and he told her that he had a sense that said, "This book has started." A few days later, an unknown copy editor left a flyer in his mailbox.

As with all spirit-filled decisions, this all bore fruit with the culmination of the product which you now hold in your hands. It is no wonder that the genesis of this book is hinged on faith, which is its pivotal theme. The life experiences which are related here are a testimony to the patience that is necessary with the often slow evolution of God's plan.

In a world which rejects suffering and demands immediate solutions, this story invites you to see the presence of God in times of both trial and celebration, if only we embrace all situations with trust in the plan of a Father who loves us deeply and unconditionally.

Linda Aboud Stephen

A Word from the Editor

I t was truly an inspiring experience to meet Mona Hadeed. She possesses a deep faith that many of us are still trying to cultivate for ourselves. Faith has taken a new meaning for me: it is the ability to see beyond everything in the physical realm.

Despite the trials that she and her family have faced, Mona embodies a strong pillar of faith and hope. Courageous and warm-hearted, she has an amazing spiritual tenacity. It has been such a privilege to work with her. *The Healing Desert: In the Sands of Time* is a reminder to all of us that we can't really build true faith when everything is always rosy and dandy.

To the struggling man, woman, or child: It does not matter how big your problem appears to be. You too can develop and strengthen your faith, if you dare not give up and trust in God. I bear witness to the fact that faith *does* move mountains.

A special message to Mona: on behalf of every reader who has been touched by your work, including myself, and the many more who will read your powerful message, I want to express sincere thanks to you, for using your life's story to show us how to create miracles in our lives.

Megan Wilson

The Desert Message to Readers

I have tried, in my writings, to put my feelings into poems, and I pray that you are able to capture the messages in between, knowing that *our God never fails us.*

I pray too that they would minister to the depths of your being, the place where the heart of Jesus dwells.

I have included different prayers and excerpts from other books and writers who ministered to me as I wrote. Over the years, I collected numerous little readings that touched me and helped me understand that I'm not alone in my trials and sufferings. I have also included scriptural verses from the Revised Standard Version of the Bible.

Let go and let God.

One spiritual writer wrote, "We look backwards in order to go forward."

Professor Timothy George

"After this I will return, and I will rebuild the dwelling of David, which has fallen; I will rebuild its ruins, and I will set it up" (Acts 15:16).

Introduction

As I share my journey of faith with the world, I realise and understand that God Himself has given me the life that I have so that my experiences will help me to guide others on their journey.

I am often reminded in my journey about *The Wounded Healer*, a book by Henri J.M. Nouwen.[5]

It's only when we have been wounded that we understand another's desert path and can draw strength from the crucified Christ.

The story of the butterfly reveals to us what we can encounter, if we do not let God have His way.

---

[5] Henri J. M. Nouwen, *The Wounded Healer: Ministry in Contemporary Society.* London: Darton, Longman & Todd, 1994.

A Butterfly

A man found the cocoon of a butterfly that was about to emerge. He sat and watched the butterfly for several hours as it struggled to force its body through that little hole. Then, it seemed to stop making any progress. It appeared as if it had gotten as far as it could and could go no further.

So the man decided to help the butterfly. He took a pair of scissors and snipped off the remaining bit of the cocoon. The butterfly then emerged easily—but it had a swollen body and small, shrivelled wings. The man continued to watch the butterfly, expecting that, at any moment, the wings would enlarge and expand to be able to support the body. Neither happened. In fact, the butterfly spent the rest of its life crawling around with a swollen body and shrivelled wings.

It was never able to fly.

The man, in his kindness and haste, did not understand that the restricting cocoon and the struggle required for the butterfly to get through the tiny opening were Nature's way of forcing fluid from the body of the butterfly into its wings. This ensures that it will be ready for flight once it achieves its freedom from the cocoon.

Sometimes struggles are exactly what we need in our life. If we were allowed to go through our life without any obstacles, it would cripple us. We would not be as strong as what we could have been.

We could never fly.

> I asked for Strength . . . And I was given difficulties to make me strong.
> I asked for Wisdom . . . And I was given problems to solve.
> I asked for Prosperity . . . And I was given brain and brawn to work.
> I asked for Courage . . . And I was given danger to overcome.
> I asked for Love . . . And I was given troubled people to help.
> I asked for Favours . . . And I was given opportunities.
>
> I received nothing I wanted. I received everything I needed.

Author unknown

I finally came to understand that the trials and tribulations, sorrows and joys, are the catalysts that draw us closer to God and His Son, Jesus, who also endured suffering in His life; for He has been my teacher, and through Him, I learned how to fly.

Chapter 1

The Awakening

The Faith Journey Begins

A THOUGHT REMEMBERED: 1978

While writing this book, my memory was jolted by the Holy Spirit, and I realised that I was meant to include this introductory story. Unknowingly, I had already begun my journey of deep faith in God, and it was the start of my witness of His gift of faith to me. This is how my faith was deepened and nourished—through my commitment to prayer and listening to the voice of His spirit talking to my heart.

When I visited my sister abroad with my little son, I became concerned about a growing lump that suddenly appeared on my neck. When I visited the doctor, he recommended that I have it removed. It turned out to be toxoplasmosis, a viral infection that can be contracted from cats and dogs.

There was no life-threatening danger; however, it could have posed a risk to an unborn baby, which raised the question of whether I was pregnant or not. To my knowledge at the time, I was not. As time passed by, after returning home, I found out that I was, in fact, pregnant. Concern arose from my doctor, and I was sent for further blood testing, which would reveal if it was an old viral infection or an active one. The results showed that the infection was active, which meant that I had only contracted it recently.

I was told that the only option was to have an abortion, because there was a risk that the fetus might not develop properly in the womb. The doctors took for granted that I would agree. To their surprise and amazement, I was not in favour of their advice. Although I was not as deeply rooted in my faith as I am today, something deep inside of me revolted the idea, and I could never consent to making a decision like that. The doctors were astounded and tried to convince me to abort because they could not imagine that I would risk having an abnormal child. Back then in the 70s, we didn't even have the updated medical equipment that doctors use today to help women through uncertain pregnancy decisions.

My husband Aziz and I loved children, and we were happy for this gift given to us. It was impossible for me to imagine having an abortion, and I began my prayer:

"God, if there is anything wrong with my baby, let me abort naturally."

When I was in the process of writing this book, the Lord reminded me of that point in my life, and as I reflected, the whole picture came together. The Lord had begun the preparation in the life of my faith journey, and thirty-five years later, I saw how the Master's plan unfolded.

What a mighty God we serve!

For the first few months of my pregnancy, my family doctor and other doctors encouraged me to reconsider; they tried to make me see what could happen to the baby. I remain rooted in my decision and thoughts. During the nine months of a pregnancy that the doctors were fearful about, my prayer remained the same.

Each time I visited the doctor, he could not fathom why I was so calm about it. Little did I know that God had begun strengthening my faith, and I was an instrument in His hand! I only had to respond—*and I did.*

The time came for the birth of my baby, and after hours of labour, I had to have a caesarean section, as I was not able to give birth to her naturally.

When I awoke after the surgery, my beautiful baby girl was placed on top of me and I cuddled her, gazing upon our precious gift. She was the most perfect little girl and so beautiful. The doctor looked at me, and all he could say was, "For nine months, you've made me tremble with fear and worry."

God had shown His power and glory, and my faith and trust in the Healing Desert of nine months had proven that **"if you have faith as small as a mustard seed, you can say to this mountain, 'Move from here to there,' and it will move. Nothing will be impossible for you"** (Matthew 17:20).

I had begun my first witness in faith and trust for the Lord. Today, my daughter is as beautiful as she was at birth; she is married with two children and is a teacher for children with special needs. She has a heart of gold and is a very caring and loving person.

If I had listened to the doctors, I would have been robbed of a soul God had created to love and serve Him in His broken little ones.

I give thanks to God, for giving me grace and strength in the days when I only had just a little faith. I'd like to paraphrase the late Pope John Paul II, who often encouraged young people to realise that they each had a purpose in this life:

"Discovering God's will for your life is a fascinating challenge that requires trust. Everyone has a vocation, because God has something in mind for everyone to do. True happiness is found by generously giving oneself to the Lord. Our deepest desires are signals of God's will for us. God is the one who has placed those aspirations in our hearts and as we pray, God unfolds and guides us through His purpose and truth."

MAY 1983

Where It All Began

My spiritual journey with the Lord began thirty years ago, when I was diagnosed with Hodgkin's disease—a type of cancer. Today, I look back on that journey and remember the story of the Prophet Jonah in the whale's belly. As a prophet, Jonah was called by God to deliver His message to the city of Nineveh. However, Jonah was reluctant to do so and mistakenly thought that he could run away from God. As a result of this, he was forced to recognise God's power when he was swallowed by a whale and remained in its belly for three days. Jonah then repented, thanked God for his life, and did as God asked of him. Like Jonah, I had been chosen to witness and proclaim God's power for His glory, and He was going to prepare and groom me to be a tower of faith, starting with the terrifying situation of dealing with this illness.

The first three months of facing this illness shaped my life with the Lord, which changed the values and meaning that I once had of life. At thirty years old, I was in my prime. I had three beautiful children, between the ages of four and nine years old. I was physically fit and an active member of my children's school fundraising committee, as well as my cultural club.

I was quite happy; I thought that life couldn't get any better. Spirituality was the furthest thing from my mind. Like many people, I would say I was a "Sunday Catholic," going to church whenever I could, but not really making any great effort to do so. I thought that I was teaching my children to be good and to follow the rules—but whose rules, I wondered.

It all began with a swelling under my right armpit, accompanied with a severe skin allergy, which started to worsen and become unbearable. After taking medication under my doctor's supervision for a week, there was still no improvement, so he decided to drain the lump that had grown under my arm.

I was hospitalised to have the procedure done, but what appeared to be a lump was in fact not a lump, and tissue samples were taken and sent for testing. The results were far from what I expected to hear. I was visited by a family doctor who gently broke the news to me: the biopsy results confirmed that I had Hodgkin's disease. It was the first that I had ever heard of this condition, so he patiently explained it all to me. My husband and I decided that we should travel to the United States for a second opinion.

I began an uncertain medical journey, with great doubt and trepidation. I entered the hospital, where the doctors began a series of tests to find out what I was really dealing with. Halfway into my test, I was told I had third stage Hodgkin's disease and a tumour the size of a fist in my stomach. Reality set in.

Having done all of the routine checks, a bone marrow test, scans, x-rays, and all the procedures involved with the medical routine of diagnosis, my illness was confirmed. The doctors then discussed a series of treatments with me.

I then had to decide if I would consent to a trial therapy of either only radiation, or both radiation and chemotherapy. The decision was mine to make; my name would be slotted into a machine and the answer would come.

At this point, I said to myself, "How could I *not* consider this experiment?" I was facing death and couldn't bear the thought of allowing this disease to deprive my young children of their mother. Who would take care of them and be there when they need a mother's love and comfort? Oh, how it hurt! I felt like my heart was being wrenched out.

So of course I agreed to the experiment. Just a few days later, I returned to the hospital to begin treatment.

Back at home in Trinidad, my friends and family engaged in ceaseless prayer and visited different churches, pleading for God to spare my life. Someone challenged me to pray for a miracle, something so far removed from my prayer life.

I remember leaving the hospital with Aziz at my side, and for the first time in my busied life, I noticed the trees, the sky, and the magnificent nature that surrounded me. Maybe, just maybe, I could soak it all in, and the tears welled up inside me as I saw my world crumbling right before my eyes. I looked up at the sky and knew what it was like to experience the Lord walking with me. I can still remember the picture so clearly. Jesus was above me in an image, with open arms, taking every step with me.

I did not know it then, but He was reassuring me of His presence, which has always been with me.

All weekend I prayed, "Lord, when I return to the hospital, let the doctors say that they made a mistake and that the tumour is no longer there." The simplicity of my prayer request reminded me of the Biblical scripture, **"Truly, I say to you, unless you turn and become like children, you will never enter the kingdom of heaven" (Matthew 18:3).** I prayed for a miracle, asking God to turn things around for me.

Little did I know, God was about to reveal His power, and my life would now belong solely to Him—to be shaped, pruned, nourished, and enriched with a faith needed to respond to the call He sent out to me.

It was a Tuesday when I returned to the doctor to start my treatment. There was such heaviness in my heart. The doctor greeted me as I entered his office. He seemed apologetic, and I couldn't help but notice his cheerfulness. Dare I think what raced through my mind at that point?

"Mrs. Hadeed, Mrs. Hadeed," he said, "I have good news for you." He then pointed to the films of the scan he had taken of my stomach days before.

"Look," he continued, "what I thought was a fist-sized tumour in your stomach is actually a group of air bubbles in your intestines." What a difference from what I had been told days before! I silenced his explanations, because without doubt, God had answered my prayer and those of my family and friends.

I had just experienced the first miracle in my life.

However, it was not to end just yet. I had to continue medical screening, and my spleen needed to be removed. I received six weeks of radiation. It was this experience that began my relationship with the Lord.

The Bible says, **"For from Him and through Him and to Him are all things. To Him be glory forever. Amen" (Romans 11:36).**

I underwent surgery and had to deal with much suffering and pain, which was further intensified as I started my six weeks of daily radiation. Every kind of support imaginable came to me from my friends and family. It was truly a time when I realised how much people in my life do care for me. Everyone rallied around me to help me through this time and illness, not knowing how it would all end. My sisters and brothers all came together to help at home with my children, trying to replace the missing link of both parents and to ensure that the children were well taken care of. Their words of comfort and consolation carried me too. My mother spent some time with me while I had my surgery and recovery. How grateful I was for having them around.

Each day, Aziz drove me to the hospital to receive my radiation treatment. God knows how grateful I was to have him by my side. I remembered those days as if they were yesterday, laying in the back seat of the car, sick to my stomach from the treatment, holding onto my pillow for comfort, and tormented by all the thoughts that raced through my mind.

Further into my treatment, my hair at the back of my head began to fall out, from the radiation. Thank God for small mercies, but it was still such a humbling experience to walk around with only half a head of hair. Too often we are so concerned with the outer beauty, but God was showing me that it's the heart of a person that mattered. I had to take my eyes off my outer self to work on my inner soul.

At different times of this journey, there were people who came into my life, and I call them angels. Thankfully, they were sent by God to help me along the way. One such angel was a tremendously strong pillar and guiding force for me, unknown to her. She was always present to help in any way and made being away from my siblings much easier. She left no stone unturned to make our stay in the United States comfortable, while I was undergoing my treatment. We don't realise that when we extend our hands and go beyond ourselves, we can heal many wounds. She gave me a card with words that became my lifeline during this time. It read:

Promise Yourself

"Promise yourself to be so strong that nothing can disturb your peace of mind.
To talk health, happiness, and prosperity to every person you meet.
To make all your friends feel that there is something in them.
To look at the sunny side of everything and make your optimism come true.
To think only of the best, to work only for the best, and to expect only the best.
To be just as enthusiastic about the success of others as you are about your own.
To forget the mistakes of the past and press on to the greater achievements of the future.
To wear a cheerful countenance at all times and give every living creature you meet a smile.
To give so much time to the improvement of yourself that you have no time to criticise others.
To be too large for worry, too noble for anger, too strong for fear, and too happy to permit the presence of trouble."[6]

Christian D. Larson

---

[6]   Christian D. Larson, *Your Forces and how to Use Them.* 1st ed. Chicago: The Progress Co. 1912.

I remember one day, feeling so sick and worn out that I wondered if I could go on any longer. I had just received a call from a good friend, who encouraged me to call on the name of the Lord. I had recently been given a Bible, and this companion was sitting on my nightstand; I picked it up and said to the Lord, "Speak to me."

As I opened the Bible, I came upon the following passage: **"Count it all joy, my brethren, when you meet various trials" (James 1:2).**

I got an unbelievable amount of consolation from this passage, and I received the grace to endure.

Suffering took on a new meaning, and I now understood the passion of Jesus and what it meant to suffer with Him and for Him.

St Therese of Lisieux once said of Jesus:

"I assure you that it costs Him dear to fill us with bitterness, but He knows that it is the only means of preparing us to know Him as He knows Himself, and to become ourselves Divine!"[7]

Finally, the six weeks of my treatment ended and I could return home to Trinidad, to my children, family, and friends. My welcome home was overwhelming, and everyone I met, I greeted with the love of Jesus, because this was the true meaning of life and fellowship.

My illness had taught me the real truth of loving with the heart of Jesus.

My faith and trust had grown in leaps and bounds, and as I started this new chapter in my life, my old way of living was behind me. I surrendered my life completely to the Lord.

---

[7]   John Beevers, *The Autobiography of St. Therese: The Story of a Soul*. New York: First Image Books Doubleday, 1987.

CHAPTER 2

Working in His Vineyard

Formation of Prayer Group

In my absence, there was a group of family and friends who had decided to come together and pray for me. My test of faithfulness and commitment to the Lord, to keep this promise until he was ready to challenge me in another direction, had just begun. Together, we chose the name, "Holy Family Prayer Group," and every Monday morning we gathered together to give thanks, to praise, to intercede, and to make reparation to God. During this time, many people crossed our path to help us grow spiritually, as we hungered for the Lord in a new way.

Our numbers grew, sometimes as many as sixty people, and the bond we shared, praying and fellowshipping together, was a taste of what Heaven could be like.

We were one in spirit, sharing each other's joys and burdens, crying and laughing together. We witnessed many miracles among us, and the Lord moved in a powerful way in all of our lives. Some of us were open to his promptings, and others were more timid.

We made some lasting friendships and were constantly meeting new people as we stayed faithful to our promise, to meet and pray every Monday. Little did we know how much we would each be called to do in so many different ways.

A Call Within the Call

SEPTEMBER 7, 1991, 11.45 P.M.

One night in prayer, these prophetic words came to me:

"My daughter, I have called you to a special vocation, one that many would not understand, but in the depth of your heart, you alone know and have realised that I have equipped you.

"For the task ahead is hard, but you can weather the storms.

"Stay close to my Sacred Heart and my Mother's Immaculate Heart, for you will feel some uncertainty, but stay steadfast for the victory will be mine.

"Put on the armour, so that you will not feel the hail that will fall upon you, but clothe yourself with my armour and you will be protected.

"Speak truth at all times and do not shy away from what I expect of you, for to whom much is given, much is expected."

Deep Spiritual Friendship

Our prayer group continued, and I grew closer and closer to one of my childhood friends, who led our group's music ministry. Then one day, I received a call that she had been in a tragic accident and would probably not survive. I rushed to the hospital, where I met with her family members, who were all in a daze. She had just passed away. I did not make it in time to see her. Her life of thirty-seven years was gone like a puff of wind.

It was the beginning of a new chapter in my spiritual life. Our friendship had grown deeper with our love for the Lord. She was one of the founding members of the group that had come together to pray for my healing. As children, we lived next door to each other, and since then, we've always had a special bond.

We never knew that God would bring us together years later, in a deeper way. She became the leader of our music ministry in our prayer group, and together we led, as we all searched for the Lord.

This deep pain in her death gave birth to yet another lasting and beautiful spiritual friendship with someone whom the Lord had placed in my path, during the nine days of prayer that we had for her. My heart ached so much for the loss of her precious life.

From Death to New Life

During one of the prayer nights, I cried out in emotional pain, and the hand that reached out to console me was like a touch from Heaven. From that moment, I knew that God had ordained this new friendship and poured His blessings upon us both.

I remember experiencing the walls around me crumbling and tumbling down. I was no longer able to hide those feelings from the world. I had become weak and vulnerable. The strong person I knew I was no longer existed. I remember dealing with decisions in that friendship, which required a strong faith and often called me beyond human understanding.

This gave birth to the wondrous work of the call of God:

To be obedient to God and not man.

All of my spiritual and physical trials have taught me many lessons in humility, true compassion, and understanding.

Most of all, the revelation of what it really meant was **"to worship the Father in spirit and truth" (John 4:23).**

As with every pain and struggle we encounter in our spiritual and daily life, we have to find a way to go on. Knowing God, and being united with His spirit, gives us the courage to move forward.

The New Call Revealed

We realise that we depend not on human strength, but the power of the Lord, who can move mountains. I continued to serve God's people and lead our prayer group, even though part of me was gone with the loss of my dearest friend. I found myself going deeper and deeper in prayer, seeking God's guidance, His vision for our prayer group, and His will for my life.

At 5 a.m. on February 4, 1992, these prophetic words came to me:

> *"Forever know this, you are called beyond human understanding, for my angels go before you and the work you must do, no other can do. Trust me explicitly, for I go before you, just unbend and the way will open before you.*

> *"Fear not the words of men for they cannot harm you, or your followers. I have covered you all with the crown of salvation, which no human nor principality can take from you.*

> *"Follow the leadings of your heart and trust that I'm speaking through your heart to you. Keep your face pointed towards me, and you will be sure to succeed.*

> *"Lead the people I send your way, for I have appointed them to journey with you. For unto us a child is born.*

> *"Just unbend. Your angel prays for you."*

Growing in the spirit and discovering Jesus in a personal way opened new dimensions in my life, both in my family struggles and in the prayer group.

God kept calling us into a deeper union with Him, and His mission for us became clearer and clearer. Our prayer group was being called to be a Eucharistic people.

Clearly, the Lord was saying that for these times, it was important for us to adore in His presence. It would be a place where we would receive strength, healing, wisdom, and insight for the present trials and knowledge of all darkness.

We embarked on erecting a Eucharistic chapel on the church grounds, where people could come at any time to sit in the presence of the Lord and be comforted and consoled, while making reparation, seeking intercession, and adoring Jesus as King and Lord.

This mission was to take me deeper into the wounds of Jesus, for I had to endure many misconceptions and hardships. I even lost friendships and was separated from many who did not understand the call of God for our group.

This is a prayer I began saying daily at the time, based on Colossians 1:9-14:

> *"I ask God that through perfect wisdom and spiritual understanding I should reach the fullest knowledge of His will. So I will be able to lead the kind of life which the Lord expects of me. A life acceptable to Him in all its aspects; showing the results in all the good actions I do and increasing my knowledge of God. I will have in me the strength based on His glorious power, never to give in, but to bear anything joyfully, thanking the Father who has made it possible for me to join the saints and with them to inherit the light. Because this is what He has done, He has taken us out of the power of darkness and created a place for us in the Kingdom of the Son that He loves and in Him we gain our freedom, the forgiveness of our sin."*

As time passed, we continued praying for guidance and waited for the Lord to move us in the direction of His Eucharistic heart.

CHAPTER 3

Journey into the Desert

FEBRUARY 1993

The Turning Point

The turning point in my life came when Aziz was diagnosed with cancer in his left kidney and a variant of hairy cell leukemia.

Dealing with this news, knowing that I would have to help Aziz to cope with it, and what could lie ahead was surely going to be a trying time. Changes in every way had to be considered, and negative thoughts and fears rolled in.

I felt like I was going through a forest with so many tall and strong trees, all of which seemed to close in on me and block the path that was before me, hiding the light I could see at the end of the clearing.

A path that I once knew was the sure way to go was now out of sight. Now, uncertainty was setting in, and I wondered, "Which way do I go?" Yet, deep within me, I saw the road clearly before me. Would I be able to overcome the boulders that just seemed to make me stumble? My view of the road ahead was different from how others saw it. Would God light that way, which now seemed to be dark? Would I be courageous and strong enough?

The world was saying one thing, clamouring out sounds, ideas, and solutions, all of which were fruitless to me, yet seemed right to the logical mind. But the mind of God was focused elsewhere. I wondered, Can the world see it, or do I have to bear it silently? Surely, life is more than the crowdedness of all that is around; who would understand what true spiritual peace is?

Is the uncertainty in my heart fear of the voices, or is it fear of letting go of what I think is beautiful, fruitful, and the way of the Lord? With His divine touch, He brightens the way, and to each step that we approach, the other becomes clearer.

We are given strength to continue, knowing that though we are scratched and torn by the brambles that tear at our skin, God's sweet, loving balm heals our wounds.

I journeyed through that long dark way, but deep within me, there was a light that was burning brightly, a light that showed me the way, even if other travellers didn't see, for as sure as my vision was, so was the landing that the naked eye couldn't see.

May God shield me from the pain and voices of the world, I prayed. I knew that God's love for me would overcome all.

What about all the ministries that I was involved in? I felt so sure that God could not be calling me to give them up. Yet Aziz needed me to be at his side. I had to be available at all times to him, dying to self and doing things I would rather not do. As Our Lord said to St Peter, **"Truly, truly, I say to you, when you were young, you girded yourself and walked where you would; but when you are old, you will stretch out your hands, and another will gird you and carry you where you do not wish to go" (John 21:18).**

"What does God really want of me?" I asked myself. I knew the answer, but why was it so difficult to surrender to His will? What about the state of the world and the message of repentance? How could I get Aziz to understand the changes he, too, must make? Many times, we believe we are the saviours of the world, and yet all we are called to do is pray and surrender to God.

The months back in the United States, away from home, facing all his tests, surgeries, and recuperation, were deeply spiritual ones for me. Graces poured out upon us from the many prayers and masses that were said for Aziz and me, by family, friends, and the prayer group.

During this time of testing, we witnessed nothing short of a divine intervention. As I prayed through it all, what appeared to be life threatening took a turn for the better.

The doctors were baffled. To God be the glory!

I had many lonely moments, with nothing to do but pray and meditate, supporting Aziz through his pain and illness, and not receiving any appreciation. During his illness, I prayed **Psalm 86:7, "There is no God to compare with You, no achievement to compare with Yours." Psalm 86: 10** says **"You alone are great, You perform marvels, You God, You alone."**

I realise more than ever now that my faith and hope that had grown over the years had prepared me for this time of doubt and anguish.

Romans 15:10 says, **"May the God of hope fill you with all joy and peace in believing, so that by the power of the Holy Spirit you may abound in hope."**

Unable to attend to a church, I had a yearning to receive Jesus and sit with Him in the Blessed Sacrament. There was much inner turmoil of the uncertainties ahead and the changes to come.

I had many moments of feeling forgotten and cast aside, no regard for my pains and emotions at this time. Self-pity took hold of me.

It was such an appropriate time to unify myself with Jesus on the cross. Coincidentally, it all began on the first day of the Lenten season in the Catholic Church. I began to experience Jesus' Calvary.

Being ridiculed, stripped, beaten.

The journey of His passion and death.

I now await His resurrection, as day by day, I see His glory shining through.

At that time, I also began a thirty-three-day consecration to Jesus through Mary by St Louis de Montfort. I can say that I experienced thirty-three days of mortification.

MARCH 1993

The Beginnings

I feel like I'm going through a forest, with so many tall, strong trees, all which seem to close in on me; blocking the path that I see before me,
Hiding the light I see at the end of the clearing.
A path I once knew was the sure way to go
Now uncertainty is setting in and I wonder which path I should follow
Yet deep within me I see the road clear before me.
Would I be able to overcome the boulders that crowd me?
My view of the road ahead will not be as others see.
Would God light that way which seems now to be dark?
Will I be courageous enough to be as strong as I should be?
The world is saying many things, clamouring out sounds, ideas, solutions, all of which are fruitless to me, yet seem so right to the naked eye.
But the eye of God was pointing elsewhere.
Can they all see it, or do I have to bear it silently?
Is the uncertainty in my heart fear of the voices?
Or is it fear of my letting go what I think is beautiful, fruitful, and the way of the Lord?
Surely life is more than the crowdedness of all that surrounds us.
Who would understand what true spiritual peace is?
Living in the presence of the love of the Almighty that walks hand in hand with you, as you journey through the forest in **the Healing Desert in the Sands of Time**.
With His divine touch He brightens the way, and to each step that we approach the other becomes clearer.
We are given strength to continue knowing that though we are scratched and torn by the brambles, God's sweet, loving balm heals our wounds.
I journey through that long, dark way, but deep within me there is a light that is burning bright, a light that will show me the way, even if other travellers don't see it.
For as sure as my vision is, so is the landing that the naked eye can't see.
May God shield me from the pain and voices of the world; for this, I'm sure, God's love for me overcomes all.

Mona

PRAYER

My Lord God, I have no idea where I am going. I do not see the road ahead of me. I cannot know for certain where it will end.

Nor do I really know myself, and the fact that I think that I am following your will does not mean that I am actually doing so.

But I believe that the desire to please you does in fact please you, and I hope I have that desire in all that I am doing.

I hope that I will never do anything apart from that desire, and I know that if I do this, you will lead me by the right road.

Though I may seem to be lost and in the shadow of death, I will not fear, for you are ever with me and you will never leave me to face my perils alone.[8]

Thomas Merton

The Mustard Seed

"The mustard seed . . . is the smallest
Of all seeds,
But when it has grown,
It is the greatest of shrubs
And becomes a tree,
so that the birds of the air come and make nests in its branches."

"If you have faith as a grain of mustard seed . . .
nothing will be impossible to you."

Matthew 13:31-32, 17:20

---

8   Thomas Merton, *I Have Seen What I Was Looking For.* Hyde Park: New City Press, 2005.

APRIL 2, 1993

The Blizzard

Out of the depth I cry to you dear Lord—alone, lonely, single, and forsaken.
Fill the very fibre of my being; satisfy my every need, for only the breath
of your spirit supplies my every desire.
Where, God, are you as I cling to your promises, the source of my comfort?
Again Lord, you test me and I surrender to your moulding
I see your gentle hand forming me
But oh! What pain to endure!
Uprooted, tossed about, tried, and discarded
Lord, who can really know what I had to endure? Only you truly see
But all for you I bore it, knowing that you will not forsake me, just as your
Father did not forsake you in the garden of Gethsemane. For I know that
every Gethsemane is your garden.

Mona

Prayer in Time of Suffering

Lord Jesus, sometimes my pain consumes me so completely that I feel as
if I have little to offer to the Father, except my suffering.
I know that you are with me in this, for you also knew pain, loneliness,
and the sense of being abandoned.
Yet I do not always reach out in prayer.
Because it is so difficult for me to pray, I ask you
to be with me even when I am not aware of your presence, and
to join me in bringing my suffering to the Father, as you bought yours to
Him in Gethsemane.
Help me to place my whole self in the Father's hands, as you did on the
cross.
Father, into your hands I entrust my spirit.

Mona

APRIL 3, 1993

God's Bubbles

Amidst this desert darkness, I see a light.
Lord, it's the light of laughter and friends—
People whom you send to lighten the day.
Friends that are precious pearls, gifts from heaven who brighten the day and hold your hands.
One whose hug embraces the pain and pours healing love, care, and concern on these open wounds.
As sure as your word says in the book of Sirach: **"A faithful friend is a sure shelter, whosoever finds one has found a rare treasure and whoever fears the Lord will find one"** (Sirach 6:14).

> God, I thank you for the friends I have found—priceless pearls,
> Pearls that glitter in the darkness; their laughter penetrates the thickened walls.
> One whose insight touches and eases my pain.
> Lord, I know you are near by the friends that are mine, gifts given to me, handpicked by you—Father, Son, and Holy Spirit—Trinity, one love,
> A love that knows no bounds.
> Thank you, Lord, that I can feel that Trinity love in my God-given friends.

Prayer to the Trinity

> Father, continue to hold me and all creation in your loving hands,
> Jesus my brother, Son of the Father, walk with me:
>> before me, to guide me,
>> behind me, to shield me,
>> beside me, to support me and be my companion.
> The Holy Spirit surrounds me and fills me with the fire of love and the breath of life.
> I praise you, Father, Son, and Holy Spirit.
> Amen.

Mona

April 4, 1993

Sunshine

Good morning, Jesus, the sun is shining today, the birds are chirping sweetly,
Nature cries out the wonder you are.
Today my burden feels light,
Hope is burning bright, yes I will survive today.
The sun pours down your graces as I delight in the warmth of your touch.
I have strength to carry on and still, though there is uncertainty, you stand in the distance beckoning,
Come on, my child, I am at the end of this journey.
Oh, what gladness my heart feels today, for there is joy in my suffering—
for so too you did endure.
My God, I am one with you; gladness fills my heart.
The sun is shining, the birds are chirping, the cool breeze is like a blanket over me.
Lord, I am free—my suffering has found its purpose.

Mona

Praise to God

"You are holy, Lord, the only God, and
Your deeds are wonderful.
You are strong,
You are great,
You are the most high,
You are almighty,
You, Holy Father, are king of heaven and earth.
You are three in one,
Lord God, all good.
You are good, all good, and supreme good.
Lord God, living and true,
You are love,
You are wisdom, you are humility,
You are endurance, you are rest,
You are peace, you are joy and gladness,
You are justice and moderation,
You are all our riches and you surface for us.
You are beauty, you are gentleness, and you are our protector,
You are our guardian and defender, you are courage,
You are our heaven and hope.
You are our faith, our great consolation,
You are our eternal life, great and wonderful.
Lord, God almighty, merciful saviour."[9]

St Francis of Assisi

---

[9] Theo H. Zweerman, Edith van den Goorbergh, *Saint Francis of Assisi: A Guide for Our Times.* Leuven, Belgium: Peeters, 2007

APRIL 6, 1993

The Child

Lord, today I have been tested; can past emotions cause such
pain?
Lord, I don't understand your ways.
Can you spare a sight for me?
To truly love one's brother in sin, yet to be the Christ Jesus at
the well.
How hard, Lord, to correct in love,
Understanding human frailty and weakness.
The temptations that glitter like gold—priceless but worthless.
"For what does it profit a man if he gains the whole world and
suffer the loss of his own soul?"
Lord, today I have been tested.
My friend, who passed away, has been betrayed.
Did I pass your test?
Did I see with the heart and mind of Christ?
Lord, spare my brother today; accept his love and not his act.
For a child has been born. What child is this?
Innocent, yet unknown.
Lord, I ache for the friend I lost.
Hear my cry this day, for my pain goes deep.

Mona

Spiritual Illuminations

"For it's not physical solitude that actually separates one from other men, not physical isolation, but spiritual isolation.

It's not the desert island, not the stormy wilderness that cuts you from the people you love.

It's the wilderness in the mind, the desert waste in the heart through which one wonders lost and a stranger.

When one is a stranger to oneself, then one is estranged from others too. If one is out of touch with oneself, then one cannot touch others."[10]

Anne Morrow Lindbergh

"When we walk our way and encounter a man who comes towards us, walking his way, we know our way only and not his. For his comes to life for us only in the encounter."[11]

Martin Buber

---

[10] Anne Morrow Lindbergh, *Gift from the Sea.* New York: Pantheon, 1991
[11] Martin Buber, *I and Thou.* Eastford, CT: Martino Fine Books, 2010

APRIL 18, 1993

The Deepest Desert

Oh, what wilderness I journey through this week! Lord, by what thoughts can I understand?

What appeared to be right, now seems crowded and wrong. I feel so worthless, fallen, and worm-like.

Yet Lord, I know that you are there, for it's times like these that I feel your hands moulding the hardest.

This time, not even "God's Bubbles" illumined the way.

For you too, Lord, felt angry, forsaken, unappreciated, and stripped, and still you bore it all with such humility. Now:

I have failed, Lord, more than once.

I see your pitying look upon me, and your gaze says, "My child, you know the answer.

"This is the thickest, deepest part of the forest, and this you must pass through. Lost you would become, your path way uncertain, but haven't I told you that I'm there?

"I'm not ready for you to come to me. Be patient yet a while longer. You must make the clearing for others. Pick yourself up and drink from the fountain of living waters.

"Feel my spirit refresh you yet a while longer."

Mona

APRIL 19, 1993

New Joy

Today, Lord, the news is good. I know you heard my deepest prayer, united with Mary, my mother, as I prayed to you. Answer you did, all praise to your name. The light is shining bright for my spouse today. My heart feels much joy, the trees are green, and maybe, Lord, I'm halfway there. The prayer I've found today says that you've spoken.

Mona

Prayer: Set Apart to God

Lord, today when I read in the book of Kings about the dedication of the temple, I was especially impressed with Solomon's dedicatory prayer.

He reminded me that you singled Israel out from all the nations of the world to be your own inheritance (1 Kings 8:53).

These people lived under the old covenant. How much more am I of the new covenant, singled out to be your inheritance?

How blessed I am! After the temple was dedicated, the people went home "joyful and glad in heart for all the good you had done."

How much more reason I have to be joyful for all the good you are doing! The thrill of knowing I am your purchased possession causes me to sing with the psalmist: **"Praise the Lord! For the Lord is good, sing praises to His name, for He is gracious. For the Lord has chosen [me] for Himself . . . as His own possession" (Psalm 135:3-4).**

My child, as I esteemed the prayer of Solomon that day, I also honour your prayer.

It was I who consecrated the temple of Jerusalem "by outfitting my name there forever."

In like manner I have consecrated you and set you apart for myself.

My name is stamped upon your heart as a reminder to you of my abiding presence.

I reside within you that you may be filled with joy in all you do.

I came that they may have life, and have it abundantly (John 10:10).

Be filled with gladness. Let your whole being radiate my joy.[12]

Marie Shropshire

And so, my spiritual journey continued, and the Lord allowed the paths of life to take me through the plans He had in store for me, to draw closer to Him.

---

[12] Marie Shropshire, *In Touch with God: How God Speaks to a Prayerful Heart.* Eugene, OR: Harvest House Publishers, 2005.

APRIL 23, 1993

The Separated

Lord, life seems so unfair.
Two close friends have been parted.
How can this be?
Two hearts that have become one, are separated,
Pierced through and through, knitted so closely, battered, bruised, torn open.
Can this wound really heal?
Lord, I stepped back and had to watch.
My heart felt it deep, so helpless, calling from afar.
Please don't part, one moment too late, weaved into one.
Blindness has overtaken and separation has come!
Each pained, yet one more than the other . . . battered, bruised, torn open.
Can this wound really heal?
Lord, I stepped back and had to watch.
My heart felt it deep, so helpless, calling from afar.
Please don't part, one moment too late.
God, can this be true? My good friend has parted thus.

Mona

Spiritual Illuminations

"Of those so close beside me, which are you?
God bless the ground! I shall walk softly there
And learn by going where I have to go."[13]

Theodore Roethke

---

[13]   Theodore Roethke, *The Waking: Poems 1933-1953.* New York: Doubleday, 1953

JUNE 16, 1993

The Thorn

As I continue this journey, Lord, bereavement has set in for my friend.
Can this pain be so real?
Father, can my friend so endure?
The pain seems unbearable, but Lord, I know you are there.
Can she not see it so? Her trust is weak; uphold her, Lord.
I can't bear to see her bent so low, broken and spilled out.
No one understands her pain.
Must she die for others to live?
You did that so long ago.
You laid down your life for us to live, yet life and society rob us of this.
Who can be so brave to endure as you did?
Dear Lord, this I pray: uphold my friend, for so weak is her body today.

Mona

"Grace is but Glory begun
And Glory is but Grace perfected."[14]

Jonathan Edwards

---

[14] Jonathan Edwards, *A Treatise Concerning Religious Affections.* New York: Cosimo Classics, 2007

JULY 16, 1993

Heartache

Lord, where am I today?
My forest seems ever so thick. I am being scratched and torn by the brambles.
So many big trees are closing in around me.
I'm engulfed. Lord, where is the light through the trees?
You seem so far away. My heart has been divided.
They have pierced my heart. The wound is bleeding.
My hurt is deep, please touch me now.
Today, I'm overcome with pain.
I'm separated from my other self.
Help me find my friend again; she's hidden for a while.
Will I find her once again?
Be my friend more than ever now.
Hand in hand we walk again.

Mona

Fault

"They came to tell your faults to me,
They named them over one by one;
I laughed aloud when they were done,
I knew them all so well before,
Oh, they were blind, too blind to see
Your faults had made me love you more."[15]

Sara Teasdale

---

[15] Sara Teasdale, *Love Songs*. Charleston, SC: Forgotten Books, 2012

After returning home with Aziz from the medical trip, life continued, and my spiritual journey grew deeper. I continued to discern God's will for me in all that laid before me. Embarking on a life for the Lord required faithfulness, fortitude, perseverance, and above all a deep love for my God, who has saved me and has been merciful to my family.

Living by the standards of God, and not the world, requires steadfast commitment to the call of God and not what man requires or expects.

Each day, I faced challenges in my walk with the Lord and the situations that came along the way.

CHAPTER 4

The Rugged Way

OCTOBER 13, 1993

Pilgrimage to Betania, Venezuela

This trip was one of Calvary and resurrection. The experiences I had on the trip made me recall the words of Jesus in scripture that pointed out the times we were in and what was to come.

My message was one of endurance and perseverance, becoming contemplative in the marketplace. We must be able to find Jesus in the crowdedness and not wait for the perfect setting.

We must fight against panic and confusion and follow the road at all times. There are some who would choose to go a different way, seeing and understanding only their way. God's message to me was, *"No matter the obstacles, keep going, endure to the end and choose life."*

He wanted a band of committed followers, faithful, not complaining. I felt, in the separation of the group on the night of the prayer vigil, that God wanted me there to speak to my heart.

There was a lot of hurt and misunderstanding between the groups about how we came to be separated. It seemed impossible to throw light on all the happenings, and as morning broke, we gathered to wait for the midday mass and a visit with the visionary.

The sun beat down, and the wait was long. There was much complaining and grumbling, and it seemed that everyone was angry and hurt by me. I felt that silence was what God was asking of me. I was misunderstood and knew no explanation that would be of use.

We were each called before God to heed His message and personally examine ourselves. It was hard and painful, and much growth was involved—an experience of a call to a deeper conversion.

For me, I felt myself being led into something deeper, a depth of understanding of the divine way, the interior way. Like Mary, I had to wait in silence and pain and uncertainty. The trip ended with disunity among some of us over existing problems, and it was evident that we had allowed the spirit of discord to enter.

I know that God's heart pained in all the events, but His mercy is great and the victory would be His. I suffered the insults and misjudgements for the sake of God, while uniting my pain with the pain of my other friends, who also felt humiliated, misjudged, and rejected.

I prayed that this experience would draw us closer to holiness. The times ahead were going to be hard, and we had to be strong to overcome.

To God be the Glory

I remembered, on our way back from the apparition site, the Lord silenced my tongue, and for about a day and a half, I could not speak. I withdrew within myself and allowed God to direct my spirit and show me His plans for me. It was a divine time, resting in the Lord, blocking out the noise of the crowds.

I knew what God was asking of me and how hard it would be to turn and go in another direction. I was being called to put all of my service and dedication to ensuring that a chapel would be installed, where we would have the Perpetual Eucharistic Adoration. This would mean that I would no longer be involved in the other ministries, except our Monday commitment to pray as a group.

This was a journey of deep faith, tolerance, courage, and selfless giving. I made the decision on my return and embarked on this new journey that God called me to.

As time went on, together with my prayer group, we started our new ministry to bring people to a deeper spirituality of adoring Jesus in the Blessed Sacrament. There were times when strength almost failed, yet God's grace carried me through. There were times when I gave until it hurt, but I kept going, knowing that Jesus had asked this of me, and like Him, I had to do it alone.

My love for God and the secrets He had revealed gave me the strength I needed. In the end, all that mattered was to love and adore him, and that reparation was made for the sins that wounded His heart and the heart of His Blessed Mother. People were touched, and the treasures of God's gifts flowed all around. He provided what was needed for His work to be completed.

On March 18, 1996, three years after this call, our adoration chapel was opened, and people were able to come and experience Jesus in prayer in the quiet and stillness, to pour out their pains, sorrows, and joys. There, they were refreshed, consoled, and given strength to carry on in the midst of their pain and thanksgiving. His call to me and the group was accomplished through the grace that He showered upon us. Amen.

OCTOBER 15, 1993

The Way

Lord, I have been touched deeply by your divine light.
Truth keeps pouring in.
The veil is torn.
Mankind, one and all are deceived.
How it pains to see the darkness of my friends.
Help me to show them the way. Not my sight but your light, uncovering all darkness with your supernatural light.
Do not let them fall into the pit.
Father, I love my friends; keep us united.
Let us not part, each another way.
May our final destination be all the same?

Mona

FEBRUARY 6, 1994

Perils

Lord Jesus, your turmoil continues to surround me, reaching out to grab hold of me.
In you, I'm anchored—the one who alone can steady the motion of the waters.
In the ocean of disturbed people, Lord, your peace sustains me.
Your spirit steadies my thoughts and actions.
The world seems to be carried away by the perils of the sea of emotions.
The underworld rises up to meet them.
Who will escape the jaws of death?
Is it those whose hands are strong, whose feet carry them far and wide?
Save us, Lord, from these "perils."
Let the saving net of your Mother's mantle gather us in—safe and secure:
To be washed upon the shores—the sand upon which you walk—the footsteps we could not see.
But Lord, we know that you carry us when we do not even know.

Mona

APRIL 10, 1994. MY 40ᵀᴴ BIRTHDAY

Pearls

Time has passed—so much has given birth, yet my soul soars upwards—
through thick and thin I find my rest.
God's love, keep pouring out,
Though Calvary has been felt—resurrection holds me up
God's spiritual gifts have been poured out today.
A day I rejoice—the celebration of my life.
Closer to you, my God.
Such beautiful gifts have been poured out.
What more can I feel?
Only the heights of heaven.
He showed His mercy.
I thank Him for the gift of my life, my friends, my family, and true
spiritual friends—their gift to me.
Bless, Lord, my unconditional love for you.

Mona

Spiritual Illuminations

"To yield is to be preserved whole.
To be bent is to become straight.
To be empty is to be full.
To be worn out is to be renewed.
To have little is to possess."[16]

Lao Tzu

---

[16]   Lao Tzu, *Tao Te Ching*. Shambhala; 1ˢᵗ ed. Boston, MA: Shambhala, 2007

MAY 4, 1994

Desolation

Jesus, to you I plead—take away my dismay.
The ones who love you have betrayed you.
They have entered into a den of betrayal.
They sit upon the throne—like wise men—but oh what fools.
Darkness has set in, your divine light has been dimmed.
I pain, Lord, for the spoken words,
But for you, I endure
I offer you my hurt and pain.
Turn it around that your kingdom may come.
Light conquers darkness.
Strip away the veils from their eyes, the deafness of their ears.
Your voice alone resounds—thundering throughout the earth.
For upon every earthly cry, you alone can decide, make accusation
You are the author of life and word.

Mona

Spiritual Illuminations

"There is no need to run outside
For better seeing.
Nor to peer from a window,
Rather abide
At the centre of your being,
For the more you leave it, the less you learn.
Search your heart and see
If he is wise who takes each turn:
The way to do is to be."[17]

Lao Tzu

---

[17] Lao Tzu, *Tao Te Ching.* Shambhala; 1st ed. Boston, MA: Shambhala, 2007

JUNE 7, 1994

The Budding

A new seed has been planted
A time of germinating
All is covered—the soil is prepared
A time of waiting,
Watching in silent expectation—words are not needed.
The season is changing
Would fruit come to being?
The silent pondering
The painful emotions
Yet winter must come, and then spring, summer, and autumn.
Which flower would bloom?
The richness of silence—incomprehensible
The farmer awaits the budding of a new season.

Mona

"Only when you drink of the river of silence
Shall you indeed sing."[18]

Kahlil Gibran

---

[18] Kahlil Gibran, *The Prophet*. Hertfordshire: Wordsworth Editions, 1997.

JUNE 15, 1994

Gethsemane

Jesus, I'm kneeling on your rock, in the garden of Gethsemane
Knowing what I'm about to face . . .
So many have betrayed me
But Lord, you would know—
How you must have hurt!
How can they do this?
They have hurt you so much,
Yet you have given your all.
My heart too, Lord, feels the same
Even my closest friend seemed to have betrayed me
They've been so insensitive, blinded
Self seeks to destroy
Why, Lord, have they fallen thus?
I feel I'm about to be crucified!
United with you, I die to rise again.

Mona

OCTOBER 1, 1994

Chains Broken

The Chains have been broken; one by one they fall away—
Linked together, yet separate—
The tool of prayer
Seemingly in sight: so weak, yet the strongest of all tools.
The darkness is slipping away,
Light is pouring in again.
The light of your divine face, to dispel all darkened areas.
One by one they experience your illumination.
Oh Lord, dispel completely the darkness of evil!
Your mercy resounds—the Angel Michael has conquered.
Praise is to God, who provides all.
Our hearts can sing and rejoice again.
Another path has been found in this healing desert.

Mona

MAY 17, 1995

The Merry Go Round

Time and time again, Lord, my world in you turns inside out.
This time, Lord, I'm faced with different feelings.
How do I decide what is your divine will for me now?
I feel again and again the same tune is being played by my friends
I'm beginning to mix up self-giving with your scene in the temple.
When do I turn over the table in the den of your house?
When do I be the gentle, loving, understanding person in Christ?
I'm confused now, Lord, for I see your house turning into a den of tax collectors.
Give me back my joy, which seems to elude me so often these days.
Help me, Lord, for you know my deepest desire is to love and serve you and your people, who you dwell in.
Help me also to love myself in the service of your kingdom.

Mona

God of love—Forgive!
Teach us how to truly live.
Ask not our race or creed,
Just take us in our hour of need,
And let us know you love us too,
And that we are a part of you . . .
And someday may man realise
That all the earth, the seas and skies
Belong to God, who made us all,
The rich, the poor, the great, the small
And in the Father's holy sight
No man is yellow, black, or white
And peace on earth cannot be found
Until we meet on common ground
And every man becomes a brother
Who worships God and loves each other.19

Helen Steiner Rice

---

19 Helen Steiner Rice, *Loving promises: especially for you.* Grand Rapids, Mchigan: F. H. Revell Co., 1975

OCTOBER 21, 1995

The Question

Where am I today?
No place to call my own
Invaded all around
Nowhere to call my own
My heart feels so far away
No home to rest my head
Oh! Where do I rest?
To find my best?
Bless, Lord, my works, my thoughts, my gifts.
I'm in the middle of nowhere
Lost in my own.
I wait, Lord, for you to call again
This time with new joy, new horizon,
A new birth is about to begin
I wait with great expectation.

Mona

General Contribution

It's hard for me to stay right here
    I've never known just why it's so.
But for some time I've wondered why
    My body stays while my mind goes.
It flies to my own secret place
    Far from people I have known.
When I can't bear the pain or hurt
    Where I feel safe is where I've gone.
I've often wanted to live there
    Although I'd be all alone.
It gives me peace, turns out the lights,
    And keeps my secrets still unknown.

Author unknown

SEPTEMBER 7, 1996

Declared

Beyond time and space,
Who knows the plan of the Lord?
Yet humans make to determine
Their own.
A soul chosen by God
Declared to the world,
Yet hidden by some . . .
Time evolved . . . four years passed.
God was calling . . . who will respond?
The barriers were finally broken.
God's glory shone through.
She was declared . . .
"The pearl of great price"
Ann Marie.
The show goes on . . .
Somewhere over the rainbow.

Mona

OCTOBER 1996

Going Home

Lord, when my heavenly call is come
When the light of this world is no more,
Let there be rejoicing, for I'm going home . . .
A place of no more pain and sadness.
Let earth rejoice, for there's reason to be glad.
No clothes of mourning,
But garb of pure white.
Let the sadness of my passing be within.
The world must know that my life is to be celebrated.
My children must love my memories in joy.
For black is the symbol of darkness . . .
White . . . the light of the Resurrection.

Mona

Adoration

"Jesus"
Who can comprehend the delight of your presence?
The sweetness of your fragrance,
The delight of your company,
The peace you bestow,
The joy you impart.
Oh! If only they knew what they denied themselves.
For your presence, Lord, is sweeter than honey.
I long to be in your presence . . . Daily . . .
To savour the love you pour out.
Life is worth the living, just because of you.
All that surround us becomes beauty in you.
Through the eyes you give to us.
Truly—Beauty is in the eyes of the beholder.

Mona

Reflection

Did you speak with Jesus today?
Did you sit awhile with Him?
Did you hear Him whisper to you things of yourself, your family, your neighbour?
If not, take the time to be with Him and hear him say,
"How I love you, my child; rest on my chest as my beloved John."

Mona

NOVEMBER 1996

I continued on my journey, serving the Lord in all the ways He called. I continued serving Him in the Blessed Sacrament; I diligently continued to attend to the flowers on the altar in the chapel. One day, while lovingly fixing the altar, someone handed me a note.

Mona:

"This labour of love for the Lord will bring you many blessings now and always.
"He is such a good Lord who appreciates every thought you give Him."

As time passed, that little note passed to me in the Blessed Sacrament came alive so many times, as I saw how the Lord did indeed bless me and my family. Each trial that my family experienced, though painful and fearful, we were triumphant.

FEBRUARY 20, 1997

The Wound

How painful, Lord, this journey can be!
Some are so blind, yet others see
Those friends whose eyes I thought saw,
Can they really not perceive?
Cover behind their false self
They refuse to search for the truth,
The truth that will truly let them be—simple, humble, little and poor.
The pain is immense that I encounter those friends—whom I thought saw—
But really chose to satisfy self, rather than you.

Mona

MARCH 1997

Dry Twigs

Our lives are liken to a tree
The many branches make up the years of our life—
    The different appearances,
    The lustrous leaves—the good times!
    The shedding of those leaves—the sorrows!
    The weltered branches—the hurts!
Then comes—the dry twigs—
    The unveiling of all that has been broken and hidden.
The pruning of the hand of the Master.
Once to bloom again in the beauty of the Creation.
The life of the wondrous tree will live again in the beauty of its soil.

Mona

MARCH 24, 1997

Dear Lord,

Forgive me for those times when—
Even when I feel I'm right, I act like a Pharisee.
For still in it, you call me to humility.
Help me never to make excuses for the times I may sin, just to satisfy my pleasure, my praise, and my self-importance.
Consecrate me always in your truth, that even if I have to die by the sword for truth, I will be courageous.
Stay by my side, now and always.
Blessed Mother, be my guide, my model, my inspiration, my strength.

Mona

July 23, 1997

Two Hearts

It's been some time, Lord, since heart spoke to heart.
I miss those moments alone with you—the Peace, the restfulness—just communicating—heart to heart.
My journey is twisting, winding, sometimes dark, and then brilliant with the rays of your love.
Please, Lord! May I return to the place of rest and surrender, where life is only going deeper into your heart, being one with you?

Where two hearts beat as one.

Mona

August 15, 1997

Clouded

My dearest Jesus, where once I thought the clearing was visible in the desert of my life, more brambles and thorns have sprung up.

The world seems so bent on being perfect, making life so miserable, but Lord, all you called us to be was simple and pure, loving you day by day.

Lord, I feel so weighed down, trapped, so belittled, yet loved.

I want to shed these garments that weigh me down, that prevent me from feeling the sunshine in the forest.

Do not let me be overcome by pity and sorrow, but give me grace to carry on, remembering that I can offer all to you, to be used for my sanctification and sainthood.

Mona

JUNE 24, 1998

Silence

Lord, let me not speak unless I'm spoken to
Not lead unless I'm asked to guide
Not follow unless you ask me to
Not give advice unless I'm invited to
Not offer my opinions unless I'm told to
To walk my journey guided by you—not others.
The courage to act when I know I should—for in my silence, words cannot
be understood.

Mona

JULY 10, 1998

The Density

Dear Jesus,

This desert seems to grow thicker and thicker.
How tiring the journey seems.
In the desert, there is wilderness.
The soul comprehends the love of God,
But who can understand the twists and turns?
The clearing can seem so easy to discern, but how can we with bare hands
make the clearing?
Lord, it's only you to show the way.
With your gentle hands you make all things bright and clear, the way,
your way.

Mona

AUGUST 2, 1998

Gratitude

Jesus, how fitting it is to thank you—for life—
A life that's meaningless without your life-giving breath, soaring through and in.
The beauty that you cause us to see—
Created all by you.
There to ease our burdens, cause us laughter, bring sunshine into gloom.
If only we can remove our eyes of doom—oh, to gaze at the beauty of your creation.
And blossom and bloom, where you plant us.

Mona

SEPTEMBER 11, 1998

A Loss

How can we ever understand, when you call what is your own back home?
We have given birth to them,
Loved them, nurtured them, cradled them in our—comforting arms
And when you call your own back,
How painful to let go.
Never to see that smile,
Hear that voice,
Embrace that love,
Gone forever, though just for a while,
Into the home of the one who created
Safely home, secured from all pain and hurt.
Good-bye, good-bye.

Mona

Confused

Jesus, where am I today?
What must I do?
I long for the days of old, where life was freedom to choose,
Where you occupied my every thought.
Is this the cross to bear?
The one you chose for me?
Let your voice speak loud and clear, over the hills and everywhere.
Let there be no doubt that you care for the one you love.

Mona

OCTOBER 7, 1998

Alone

Where am I today?
No place to call my own, invaded all around, nowhere to call my own.
My heart feels so far away, no home to rest my head,
Oh, where do I rest to find my best?
Bless, Lord, my works, my thoughts.
I'm in the middle of nowhere, lost in my own.
I wait, Lord, for you to call again
This time with new joy, new horizon.
A new birth is about to begin
I wait with great expectation.

Mona

SEPTEMBER 15, 1999

The Brambles

The journey continues, O Lord.
How the brambles seem to thicken as I plod along.
They seem to close in on me.
How do I see the way, which way do I turn?
The path seems out of sight.
My heart seems unsure.
Which way is the right way?
O Lord, direct my feet, make clear the way, for your sight, oh divine Master, is the sure light.
Help me discern your divine light—direct my feet.
Please show me the way!

Mona

NOVEMBER 21, 1999

The Rumble

Lord, it's that time again—I've come again to another crossroad!
It seemed so long ago that heart spoke to heart.
Did I not hear you call, or maybe I was too busy to listen to hear your voice?
Yet you gently continue to whisper as you called out my name.
Your whisper became a roar: *"I'm speaking, can't you hear?"*
"Yes, Lord," I answered, *"I've come to do your will."*
I open the door that you may enter, deeper more, I am your servant.
Behold the handmaid of the Lord, be it done unto me according to your will.

Mona

DECEMBER 6, 1998

Harmony

Life was created in harmony,
The harmony of two people's love.
A harmony that comes from a love that two agree on.
Life begins with harmony.
A hope that the two, knitted together, will bear a bond that will last forever.
"Harmony" is the thread that allows life to grow within each and every one of us.
"Harmony" is the spirit of God alive in each of us,
Yearning to reach and touch those who surround us.
"Harmony" calls us all to love in unity, hope, and care for each other.
"Harmony" calls us to put aside our fears, anxieties, jealousy, and anger.
"Harmony" is the Holy Trinity,
The Triune God,
Who united together form
The Father, Son, and Holy Spirit,
Three persons—yet one
Let us live in the spirit of "Harmony" that lives in each other, for one another.

Mona

Prayer to the Lord

Lord Jesus, I need your help to accomplish my desires.
Give me perseverance, wisdom, and discernment, to accomplish your will in my life.
Let Harmony flow, so that my spirit may be one with you.
Amen.

Mona

CHAPTER 5

His Face Reflected

JANUARY 8, 2000

Perfect Love

Great and Mighty God, I celebrate your awesome omnipotence.
You are a God of Might and Power.
From age to age, your endless love is manifested.
You are timeless for all eternity.
My heart wants to sing your greatness.
My heart desires to experience that timeless joy, which celebrates life—
2000 years ago.
Yet, I feel so imprisoned by the many stories of my life.
There seem to be no peaceful ending to the chapters.
Lord, I cry to you for the light to penetrate the darkness of misconception,
especially in those closest to me.
I only want to do your will, in your "Perfect Love."

Mona

And so, my life continued with all its ups and downs, and I clung to God's promises that He desires joy and happiness for His loved ones.

Aziz was always plagued and threatened by ill-health, yet he possessed courage and strength to survive what came his way.

We had gone for another of his medical check-ups, and this time he was told that there were benign tumours covering his liver; he had no choice but to have half of his liver removed.

Of course, this was a very serious surgery to undergo, yet we were left with few choices.

Lord, I know you are there and your love endures all.

Mona

"It's not by side stepping or fleeing from suffering that we are healed, but rather by our capacity for accepting it, maturing through it, and finding meaning through union with Christ, who suffered with infinite love" (Pope Benedict XVI *Encyclical Letter Spe Salvi*, "In hope we were saved," 37).

MARCH 20, 2000

Dear Lord,

It seems that this circle of life comes around so often in my spiritual journey.

The indecision of what is really your will for me and Aziz at this time.

We seem to always experience the power of your mercy and love.

In this time you took us even a step closer to the experience of Abraham who was called to offer up his only son.

Like Abraham, you called us to trust you in total darkness.

What is the best decision? I just can't seem to find a clear answer.

Yet my heart calls out to trust you one more step beyond.

There's so much I can fool myself with, so much that can influence my clarity and discernment.

My desire to live out my own plans, but I know I must surrender them to you, for you know best.

So Lord, I surrender, I trust you, I surrender all to you.

Mona

MARCH 21, 2000

The answer came: go forward in faith, be not afraid. Yet I wonder, what would tomorrow bring—a miracle once again?

This I know, Lord, you never fail me, and again you would show your love and mercy. All will be well and your name will be glorified.

Mona

MARCH 23, 2000

Hosanna

The day has ended, your angels sang—Hosanna to the King of Kings, let us praise Him, let us adore Him, lift up your hands and praise Him.
I have seen your glory again, Lord. Aziz has been saved one more time.
As I relive this day, trusting in you completely. I give my life over to you, all is in your hands, as I sit and wait a while.
Aziz is being operated on; the many thoughts assail me, the long hours of the unknown.
I cling to your promises, to come unto you when I'm heavy laden . . .
Yet, Lord, my heart was light, for my spirit and trust is anchored in you, my soul united to you as each hour passed.

Mona

MARCH 29, 2000: LENTEN SEASON

As I sit and ponder this Lenten season, my experiences of self-mortification and fasting were planned out for me. Not as I would have had it, but as God ordained.
I had the experience of truly offering up the sacrifices I was called to make, as I nursed and gave of myself to Aziz.
The many times that I was used as a bouncing ball, thrown from side to side.
Nothing I did was ever right, and yet I did it all out of love, care, and concern.
But I know, Lord, that this Lent, my call was to serve as Christ did: "He came not to be served, but to serve."
What a privilege to have an opportunity as Christ had to wash the feet of His disciples, even when He knew He would be betrayed by one of them.
Lord, I thank you for the call this Lenten season.
I pray that I may grow closer to you, united with your walk to Calvary, knowing that the glorious resurrection awaits those whom He calls
For there can be no Crown without the Cross.

Mona

MARCH 31, 2000

Sacrifice

Lord, today I feel so tied down, so weary and controlled, punched at and torn apart.
I carried Aziz's pains and discomfort, understanding his needs, yet reaching my end.
Nothing I did seemed right and was only met with disappointment and criticism.
I know when pain is overwhelming, those around endure the laceration.
The many times I wanted to retaliate, but I kept the thought deep within, that this Lent, my sacrifice was one of self-giving.
I kept before me your passion; it gave me strength to carry on.
If you endured—Oh, King of the Universe—such ridicule and laceration, who am I to complain?

I walk with you to Calvary and I experience the help of those who love me, as they carry me in prayer.
I know I fell a few times, but there was always a prayer to lift me up.
I feel today I've reached the destination of the cross and that final lance, pierced my side.
I surrender to this death today and know that life will rise again
A new day will dawn—another day.

Mona

APRIL 1, 2000

An Oasis of Peace

What a beautiful morning, Jesus, nature rings out your Majesty—the birds singing, bellowing such beautiful songs.
The chirping of father bird, perched above the top of the roof, announces the dawn of a new day.
I watch them fly about, so freely, so gracefully, so serene.
The sound of the air, the breeze blowing against the trees, as they sway from side to side, everything coming together to form—the Harmony of Life

The sun begins to peer through the trees, soft small clouds adorn the sky, and in the midst of it, an airplane soars high through the clouds, reminding me that man becomes part of God's creation, soaring to other destinations, hoping to find freedom, peace, and happiness.

Bless this wonderful day, Jesus; wrap us in your loving arms.
Let us feel your loving embrace, your comfort and security. I know Jesus, just as that song says, *"He's got the whole world in His hands—yes, He's got the whole wide world, in His hands."*

Thank you, Jesus, and I love you, Lord.

Mona

APRIL 13, 2000

Hi Jesus,

It's that time again as I sit and wait in hope and anticipation.
I always seem to be knocking on your door, pleading and seeking your mercy as each situation presents itself.
I surrender all my feelings, fears, and plans to your most perfect will.

Lord, your will is always the perfect will, and I trust that you will work things out for your honour and glory.
Glorify your name in Aziz; let him experience your loving, healing touch.
Answer his plea and set him free of all pain and complications.

Lord, guide the hands of the doctors as they minister their healing touch to him.
Guide their hands and protect Aziz from any further setbacks.
Jesus, you have never failed me, and most of all, Lord, I really need you now to resolve all Aziz's complications
Lord, you know my heart's desire is to walk in your footsteps in Jerusalem, where you laboured and journeyed to Calvary.
I ask you please, Lord, to open the way that I may be able to make this trip—let your holy will be done in me and Aziz.
Thank you, Jesus, for your love and mercy.

Mona

APRIL 18, 2000

Disillusioned

Dear Lord,

Days have passed, I've been so numb, such confused thoughts! What would tomorrow bring?
Each day I look for the silver lining, the sun peeping through—yet I waited in anticipation, knowing, Lord, you would not let me down.
I feel the call of Abraham, to trust in the dark, to be led, a call to believe.
Lord, I know deep down your love for Aziz and me will overcome all.

Today, Lord, I felt the sun would shine, but somehow a cloud hid its brilliance. I was faced with such indecision, as darkness loomed.
What is the right decision? Did I not want to doubt your mercy and love for us! But I felt my world come tumbling down. I battled with all my emotions; would Aziz have to be operated on again? The odds were against him; how much longer must he suffer? Yet I said, "Most Sacred Heart of Jesus, I place all my trust in you."

I prayed for the wisdom of the doctors to decide on the right approach. Oh Lord, be their guide. Come, Holy Spirit, Come.
I felt I could not bear the tension and waiting, each time he was taken for a procedure.
The time ticked away so slowly and my thoughts crowded me, yet I tried not to let my faith be shaken.
Today, Lord, I trust you as the clouds thicken.
I take up the challenge of the God of Abraham.

Mona

April 20, 2000

The Final Moment

It's that time again to sit, wait, and pray. Lord, I seem to have exhausted all words, but I know you see my innermost thoughts, fears, anxieties, and yes, even a little doubt.

My faith grew dim, but only for a moment, as I contemplate your passion and remember your glorious Resurrection.

The waiting is over, at last a word of encouragement and hope.

All went well, only patience and time, but your grace is so much needed.

Pour out in abundance upon us all, your saving grace, lessen Aziz's pain.

We all grow weary, our hands limp. Stretch out your hands and steady us as we continue this journey of waiting and healing.

We thank you, Lord, for you have heard the cries of your people, like those who lowered the stretcher for the lame man to be healed.

Please, Lord, make clear the way and give me your divine wisdom and discernment to make all the right decisions for the path ahead.

I thank you, Lord, for being there, with your Blessed Mother and all the angels and saints.

Mona

Possible Disappointment

I had signed up to go on a pilgrimage to the Holy Land in the year 2000, the Year of Jubilee. I was so excited to go because the pope at the time, John Paul II, was bestowing special blessings upon those who were in attendance; and it was also my first time going to Jerusalem and Rome. I was fearful that I might not be able to go.

It would appear that Aziz's illness and surgery required a long recuperation, and I might not be able to leave him. I had to surrender my deep yearning to visit the Holy Land and wait on God.

As the days passed by, each morning brought new feelings and thoughts, and as I tried to put them into words, consolation came as I spoke to my God for strength for the day. I share with you these feelings in the hope that, as you too experience sorrow and turmoil, you may feel comforted as I did, knowing that God never forsakes us.

This surgery of his liver was very complicated, and he experienced a lot of hardships. For five months, he suffered with the problem of a leaking bile duct, which was too risky to operate and fix. His previous surgery, where they removed half of his liver, was so life threatening that the doctors were reluctant to operate and repair it.

I prayed earnestly for the wisdom of the doctors on how best they should approach this problem. Finally it was decided to insert a tube and allow drainage to occur outwardly, while periodically administering isopropyl alcohol to the area, in the hope that it would shrink and close the open wound.

This entailed measuring the fluid output and cleaning the wound so as to avoid any infection. To God, I offered up my fears and daily struggles of nursing him and being a tower of strength for him. This continued until eventually, bit by bit, after travelling to the clinic every six weeks, the doctors decided to remove the drainage tube, and he was free again to live his life, with joy, sorrow, and fear.

Being the strong and hopeful man that he was, he focused on living and made every effort to finish the job the Lord had put him on earth for, namely, to groom his family and ensure that he taught them well and provided for them by the sweat of his brow.

He never allowed his illness to cripple him and cause him to lose hope, and he was always admired for the endurance and strength he possessed.

His humorous nature was never dampened, and he overcame his fears that he would soon die.

In the midst of this time, I was still uncertain if I would be able to make my pilgrimage to the Holy Land, and my trust and faith was tested in a deeper way.

We continued to deal with his recovery and all that took place during this healing and waiting. There were times I thought all would be well, and I could get excited about going on my pilgrimage, and suddenly he would develop an infection and things would look dim.

I remembered reading this statement once:

Disappointments

It's just God's way of saying

"I have got something better."

Be Patient . . .

Have Faith . . .

Trust God . . .

APRIL 29, 2000

Journey to Calvary

My God, you know how heavy my heart is tonight. I can hide nothing from you, for you know me through and through.

Lift the burden of my heart and help me to look beyond my hurt and pain.

Help me to look deep within and change what needs to be changed.

Do not let me look on my lack of being understood, accepted for who I am.

Don't let me find excuses for my pain, but only let me be unified with you, as I meditate on your passion and death.

Help me to die to self and be silent in my defence.

Thank you, Jesus, for your unconditional love.

Mona

I continued to pray and wait, trusting God, in the hope that maybe, just maybe, a light would shine in my thoughts and I could make the pilgrimage. I knew, too, that Aziz was reluctant to let me go, because he felt safe having me at his side. Lord, can I put aside my excitement and desire to make this trip? Yet I knew I had to truly surrender to my desire and let God pave the way and give me the grace to accept His will for me.

"Father, into thy hands I commit my spirit" (Luke 23:46).

It was only a day before the pilgrimage was scheduled that I knew I would be able to make the trip. God had ordained that I was still in Miami with Aziz, who was under medical attention, and this was the point of departure for the trip. That made it possible for me to join the group at the last moment. My daughter and sister-in-law offered to stay with Aziz while I was gone, which was yet another blessing.

God's ways are not our ways.

MAY 11, 2000

Pilgrimage to Jerusalem

With deep joy in my heart, I set out on my pilgrimage, anxious to walk in the footsteps of Jesus' journey, see His birthplace, and experience history come to life. After a week in Rome and experiencing scripture come alive, we arrived in Israel, where the heart of Christianity began. As we entered the Holy Land, a tremendous peace was felt, as at once we imagined our Jesus walking these roads.

We visited the site of Nazareth, the church of the Assumption, Mt Tabor, Capernaum Taiga (the home of Jesus), Mount of the Beatitudes, and the Sea of Galilee. Mass was said in the church of the Assumption and the Mount of Beatitudes.

Each experience was so moving, and as we embraced the moments of our Lord and Saviour, we felt our faith grow deeper and deeper; we asked God for the strength and grace to journey on in life.

We went to Cana, the hometown of St Anne and St Joachim, parents of our Blessed Mother Mary, and couples renewed their marriage vows, symbolic of the wedding feast of Capernaum.

We visited the tomb of Lazarus, and I stood outside, contemplating if I wanted to make the descent into the tomb.

Words cannot explain the feeling that overcame me. I felt something stirring up deep within me, for I had just heard that Aziz had to be taken back to hospital. As we prepared to celebrate holy mass, I united Aziz's suffering and illness with the story of Lazarus, and his sisters Martha and Mary.

As mass began, I relived the moment of Jesus with Martha and Mary; I wanted to read the liturgy of the word, and I hope that our guide would permit me to. Suddenly, I turned around and was signalled to read the first reading. It was a special moment for me, and it was two of my favourite passages on friendship: Sirach 6:1-17.

It was a moving moment, and during mass, I claimed that Aziz would rise out of his illness and come out of the tomb of darkness and depression, just as Lazarus arose out of his tomb.

The entire group of forty people prayed for him, and I know God heard our cry for his life.

MAY 12, 2000

Today was a moment in time, when 2000 years ago, Jesus walked the road to Calvary, to be ridiculed, beaten, stripped, and crucified. We followed the footsteps of Jesus on the road to Calvary, and we took turns carrying the large cross, as we partook in His journey.

It was a touching and deeply spiritual moment as my sister and I carried the cross on our shoulder and imagined Jesus walking through the streets of Jerusalem among the jeering crowds, who spat upon Him. We climbed the steps to Calvary and felt the Lord's love for us even more, as we saw what a labour of love he made for us.

It was very significant for us, as we climbed together, placing our sins and those of our ancestors on the cross, claiming freedom and life for our families and future generations.

Our trip to the Holy Land was a time stood still; scripture came alive, and the Bible was no longer a story, a tale, but a reality of life, past and present, and meeting and knowing the man Jesus. My love for Him intensified, and my desire to serve and please my God, who did all this for me, increased.

MAY 20, 2000

The Gift of Friendship

Throughout the Bible, we experience God's gifts to us in friends. We see how Jesus felt the need of having people to journey with Him, to encourage Him, and to be a source of strength for Him. While He depended on His heavenly Father for strength and courage, in His humanness, He needed the touch and love of those around Him.

His disciples were His companions and travelled with Him to the places He was sent, to minister to and heal others.

In this journey, He experienced, as we all do, the joys and sorrow of friendship, the betrayal and support, and finally, rejection and death. We are reminded that God knows our needs and always sends people to be with us on our journey in life, like Simon, who helped Jesus carry his cross.

Each friend has something different to offer, and even in this, we are called to accept and love and be a beacon of hope and life, in the midst of our own sorrows. My ordained friend, whom the Lord placed in my life after the death of my childhood friend, journeyed alongside me, and as she experienced her sufferings, I tried to keep her uplifted and secure in the arms of Jesus.

A Tribute to My Friend

I can still remember that day long ago, when something happened, time stood still, and the touch that was felt.

Something happened that no one could ever understand, except the two. Our lives were knitted in a special and divine way, a gift from above, a gift that was given by someone special who was swiftly taken away.

There began a journey in friendship, painful, yet joyful, the spirit of someone who was able to uncover all emotions that was buried from the world.

Someone who was caring, loving, free spirited, and talented.

Who can imagine a world without true friendship?
"A faithful friend is an elixir of life" (Sirach 6:16).

My friend was a friend for life, until one day, when God ordained otherwise.

"A faithful friend is a sturdy shelter: he that has found one has found a treasure" (Sirach 6:14).

Many may say, it's too painful, it's not worth it!
Many may build walls that may never crumble.

How sad it is to forfeit the union that true friends share when in company with each other!
Sometimes, no words are needed, where all pretence are shed and the masks removed, a time when just being, is to be.
A leisure moment when one can truly be real and the thoughts of each other are known.
The excitement felt when being together is enough, to watch a movie together and have a cup of coffee means so much, in this busied world.
A thought shared, a song sung, a prayer said, a wish made, the simple things that friends do to lift each other up.
Times when sadness was lessened, because someone really cared and felt your deepest pain.
A voice that comforted and gave encouragement, a strong shoulder to lean on.

"There is nothing so precious as a faithful friend, and no scales can measure his excellence" (Sirach 6:15).

Nature cries out for harmony, a world that needs friendship, a world where leaders can be friends, nations joined together, brothers and sisters loving each other.
A world where lion and cub can rest together, the birds of the air, the flowers of the field, all needing each other, to blossom and bloom.

Friendship is the picture of lives being lived, where emotions are shared, differences felt, personalities clash, hearts unite and love.

The divine Master has knitted the threads of friendship which He shared with those whom He has chosen, and there is no emotion that the Father, Son, and Holy Spirit did not feel in their union as one.

The fidelity that He kept with those who ridiculed and spat upon Him and finally betrayed Him was an example to us.

He welcomed the thief on His right and invited him to share in His glory, as at last He emptied Himself and welcomed him in.

Friendship is life shared, love broken, spilled out, and formed again.

Friendship is at the centre of life and "**whoever fears the Lord makes true friends, for as a man is, so are his friends" (Sirach 6:17).**

Thank you, my friend, for the gift that you are; for your love, care, and support; for just being you: beautiful and warm, broken and mended, for being my Sunshine, "a buttercup in bloom."

Mona

Amidst all of our journeys in life, we are called to have hands extended and not wrapped around us only. We are given opportunities to be Christ-like and help those whom God has put in our path. My journey with my friend helped me to understand that everyone is given a cross to bear, and we can become like Simon, who helped Jesus carried His cross.

JUNE 2000

Life's Twists and Turns

As I watch you, my friend, manoeuvre life with its twists and turns, I see your fears, doubts, and uncertainties.

How I long to lead you through it all, but the time has come for you to go it your way.

Mistakes you must make, wrong turns you would follow.

The pain I see you still endure, some long lost, others you must feel.

My eyes follow you and yearn to lead the way, but it's only in stumbling that you will grow. You've become stronger in many ways. I thank God for the distance you've made.

I try to walk silently behind you, though it's hard many a time. I long to see the chains that bind you broken, long to see you experience true joy and freedom.

I look at you and imagine seeing you soar on eagle's wings. What joy I feel when I imagine this happening.

I thank God for the times that I was there for you to lean your weary head on.

I thank God for the times I could ease the burdens and let you know that someone cared.

I thank God he deigned to unfold His love for you, for you are His precious gem, made to sparkle in the dark, in all the ends of the world.

My friend, as I look back on these six years, I reminisce on all the moments we've shared, precious moments, painful times, yet rich with growth.

Idle times, times when we captured the spirit of the great God who brought us together. Those deeply spiritual moments when only we knew what gift we've been given.

On this your precious milestone, I see you standing, surrounded by your life's pain, yet glowing with what lies ahead, for no doubt your Master has called you and He has a plan for you.

Like a young babe that must grow up, make mistakes, learn the lessons, and then embark on life's journey, so too I urge you to go forward in the love and strength of the great Master.

At your side I will always be, ready to hold you up when you grow weak, there to give advice, if you ask, to wipe away the tears when you cry, to applaud you when you sing, and just be there for you when you call.

May our friendship grow richer in the love of God and His Blessed Mother. May we be a beacon of light for all to see, and to Him may glory be given for the things He has done in our lives.

Mona

July 2000

Deep down inside a voice sings out the music of heaven.
A voice sings—is someone there—are you there, a voice that moans in pain and sorrow.
The night is still, the sound of music haunts the night.
A voice touched by God, blessed anointed, touched by an angel.
A voice that brings comfort in her pain and touches a soul deep within.

Mona

December 26, 2000

Dear Lord, this great Jubilee Year is coming to an end; I would have never imagined that a year that was destined to be filled with favour would end with such tragic events. Yet Lord, we embrace all the good with the not-so-good, and we know that you are with us always and there is nothing that can crumble us, once we abide in you.

Thank you, Lord, for the favours of this Jubilee Year.

Mona

MARCH 29, 2001: LENTEN SEASON

Stripped

My God, you know how heavy my heart is tonight. I can hide nothing from you, for you know me through and through.
Lift the burden of my heart and help me look beyond my pain and hurt.

Help me to look deep within and change what needs to be changed. Let me experience the hurt of not being understood and accepted for who I am. Don't let me find excuses for my pain, but only let me unified with you as I meditate on your passion and death.
Help me to die to self and be silent in my defence.
Thank you, Jesus, for your unconditional love.

Mona

APRIL 15, 2001: EASTER SUNDAY

To Be Risen

Lord, today I'm supposed to celebrate your rising from the tomb, to feel that joyous resurrection. Yet Lord, I still feel the sorrow of your Mother, who stood by silently as her son suffered His passion. I too feel that silent sorrow for my son, as I stand by silently and see him stripped, rejected, and misunderstood. His friends have betrayed him; they make a mockery of him. Lord, as I watch in pain, I yearn to defend him. I feel anger and hurt. Lord, I want to ridicule them. I know the time and the hour has not yet come. I beg your grace to wait, knowing that your mercy surrounds my son, and your grace is wrapping him like a cloak of protection. Lord, I trust in your mercy and love. I pray, Lord, that he may come to experience your all comforting, healing embrace. Jesus, embrace my daughter too, as she journeys the dark night of the soul. Let her experience a rising out of a tomb, as your resurrection rays warm her body, mind, and soul. Most sacred heart of Jesus, and Immaculate Heart of Mary, I entrust my children to you.

Mona

"Where there is love, the heart is light. Where there is love, the day is bright. Where there is love, there is a song, to help when things are going wrong. Where there is love, there is a smile, to make all things seem more worthwhile. Where there is love, there's quiet peace, a tranquil place where turmoil cease. Love changes darkness into light, and makes the heart take wingless flight.

"Oh, blessed are they who walk in love, they also walk with God above. For God is love, and through love alone man finds the joy that the saints have known."[20]

Helen Steiner Rice

"Do two walk together, unless they have made an appointment?" (Amos 3:3).

---

[20] Helen Steiner Rice, *Where There Is Love.*

NOVEMBER 5, 2002

Forgotten

Time seems to have stood still, almost an eternity has passed, thoughts come and go, none recorded—lost, stolen!
Lord, have I really not written to you for so long?
It seems to be happening again, as it did many times before.
Time and time again, I remember what you lived: rejection, ridicule, misunderstanding, and falsely accused.
I marvel at your fortitude!

Lately I seem to fall more and more under the burden of this cross.
Yet I know and hear your call: "Pick up your cross and follow me."
I'm trying, Lord, bear with me, but the thoughts are overcoming me. I'm sure you felt this way too! I know you called, "Father, take this cup come from me, not my will but thy be done."
Yes Father, I too accept this cross, help me carry it. I remember your invitation some eleven years ago, though I did not understand; I seem to have said yes.
Grant me the grace, fortitude, strength, and above all joy, because you have invited me.

Mona

JANUARY 25, 2003

Heaven

I saw a place called Heaven, where clouds were laid like blankets of snow.
A home away from home, where pain or sorrow existed no more.
A place where only sweetness flowed.
Love, pure love, care, true care.
Hope was overflowing; joy filled a heart to bursting.
A place where only laughter was heard.
No crying, no groaning, no fear, no starvation.
Oh home, sweet home.
A place to rest one's soul, all hands joined, forever praising God.
Home, sweet home.
A place called Heaven.

Mona

JUNE 2006

Creation

Forthwith the world goes;
Empty and fruitless.
As man evolves from his own being, still God creates His own destruction.
God clamours to still save,
Oh! That man would hear, see the beauty of a world once created in joy.
Destroyed by man's perception, the joy of once being:
      Purity, wholeness, and richness.
Now greed, jealousy and strife surrounds
Yet for those who can still see in the darkness of waiting, a light that dawns, a child to be born. A Saviour still to come to us, day by day to salvage a broken earth, a broken heart, a broken home.

Mona

APRIL 20, 2007

Pilgrimage to Shrines of France

Every year, our church group journeys on a pilgrimage, and I usually tried to go. That year, I was happy that God permitted me to go; life at home was uneventful. As we started out on our journey, the priest chosen to go with us gave us a message to carry with us throughout that time that we had chosen to spend with the Lord away from the busyness of the world:

"This is My Season, My Time, My Blessing."

My Prayer

Blessed Mother, I continue my commitment to you. Lead me and guide me to the heart of your son, Jesus, that together with you I would grow in holiness and strength. Lord, you are the beat of my soul. In you, I find solace and peace. Thank you for saving my life and giving me the grace to remain faithful to you. May my heart beat as one with you, as I await your glory, to see the heavens open and your glory descending. Give me a heart to understand the love that you have for me until we have a meeting of hearts.

The blessings of my children are precious pearls you've given to me. May I treasure them and keep them close to your heart and the heart of your Mother, until the day they return to you. Bless and keep them safe from all danger and harm; may they glorify you in their lives.

Amen.

Mona

I returned home and was filled with the Holy Spirit from my pilgrimage and entered into my life again as mother, wife, and friend to all. I had prayed so hard on my journey for God's blessings and protection to be poured out upon my family, and I awaited His answer to all of my desires.

I felt the deep peace of my God and an increase of my faith to face the daily events of my life and in the will of God for each day.

A few months later, we heard the good news that my daughter, Rhonda, was pregnant; profound joy filled all our hearts especially as she thought it would never happen. Aziz and I embraced this wonderful news and began anticipating the time when we would become grandparents.

CHAPTER 6

Purified in the Furnace

SEPTEMBER 2007

The Miracle Birth

The journey of faith continued . . .

Earlier on, Rhonda and Peter tried to conceive but were unable to do so for quite some years. Finally, she conceived and discovered that she was pregnant with twins! We all prayed for a safe pregnancy. Doubt set in on the success of the pregnancy because of all the difficulty they had experienced until this point.

The couple doubted . . .

How hard it is to believe without seeing, but the call of Abraham also reminds us of that unconditional trust in a Father who loves us, who wants only the best for each of His children.

A call to a deeper faith was given—the unknown for the next nine months. God was tilling the soil in preparation for the fruits of His glory. So many times we thought, would this joy be taken from us?

December 31, 2007

Unexpected Crisis

"Did I not tell you that if you would believe you would see the glory of God?" (John 11:40).

It was the last night of the year: New Year's Eve. The world was preparing its celebration to end the old and begin the new. Yes, it was a new journey, and a new year was about to begin. But I never expected it to start in a dark and frightening way. One phone call made our world stand still. Rhonda, our beloved daughter, and her babies were almost lost to us, seemingly to end as the year was ending too.

> Time stood still as the call came,
> Something was wrong:
> Only God knew!

When Aziz returned home from work, he entered the corridor of our bedrooms, and as he opened the door, he found Rhonda on the ground, semi-conscious. Fear gripped him, and he called out to our daughter Karlene and her fiancé Matthew to come quickly. They were able to place her on the bed and stood by in shock as she experienced continuous seizures. Then her husband Peter who had been called, rushed into the room to find his beloved Rhonda struggling for her life.

Meanwhile, in our humanly limitless way, we panicked and rushed to her bedside. Somehow, her life was slipping away. I poured holy water over her, praying and pleading to God to save her. I called down the divine heavenly forces, *"Lord, you are a God who saves, come, Lord Jesus, save my daughter and her little ones."*

I called Lisa, my dear cousin, and with great fear in my voice, I asked her to call an ambulance. Immediately, she left her home and encountered Dr Jackie Sabga, our family doctor, on the way over to my home. God had already begun His divine intervention. As they got to Rhonda's bedside and the doctor saw what was happening, there was a greater urgency to get her to hospital. She was having multiple seizures and possible cardiac arrest. As I watched this happening, the sight of my daughter in distress made my strength and faith grow stronger, and I begged God to act quickly. Dr Sabga realised that time was running out and we had to get her to the hospital promptly, or else she would not make it. She looked at my cousin, and they decided that they could not wait for the ambulance. Drastic times required drastic measures. The men in the family lifted Rhonda and rushed her into my cousin's car.

With my friend's skilled driving and the help of our family doctor, we got Rhonda to the hospital amidst the traffic on such a busy day. In their urgency, my cousin drove on the wrong side of the road to get to the hospital sooner. The cars were coming in her direction, and people on the road wondered if she was a woman gone mad, unaware of what was happening. At one point, she stopped the car, and Dr Sabga went out on the busy highway, waving to the other drivers to get out the way. It was like a scene from a movie, but the fact remained that they had to get her to hospital as soon as possible. I am forever grateful to them all for what they did to save her life and how God chose each person to be part of this story. Thank you, Lisa, and thank you, Dr Jackie Sabga. Thank you all.

The events that followed were unparalleled. God intervened; the Great Physician was in charge. He orchestrated the steps that were necessary to save the life of His daughter and her little ones, whom He had formed and created in her womb: the twins.

As the doctors worked out the sequence of saving Rhonda's life, God kept blocking the way. Obstacles became stepping-stones.

Our community was shaken, as people flocked to the hospital, everyone stunned, fearful of what the outcome would be on this last day of 2007.

My faith grew stronger and deeper as I called on my God, who never let me down.

I proclaimed the words over and over to the crowd, and I called upon my God, whose mercy saves, this I know.

As I knelt on my knees and prayed, the words of a song kept playing in my mind:

> *Jesus, your name is Power—*
> *Jesus, your name is Life—*
> *Jesus, your name will free every captive—*
> *Jesus, your name is Life—*
> *Jesus, your name is Glory—*
> *Jesus, your name brings Sight—*
> *Jesus, your name above every other—*
> *Jesus, your name is Life.*

Down on my knees, I prayed that song, holding the hands of my son-in-law Peter, who was shattered and losing faith. Would he lose his newly beloved?

Fear, anxiety, despair, and the thought of losing his long-awaited babies gripped him, and his world came crumbling down. I continued to pray the song and knew that God would look with mercy upon them. All of our family surrounded us, and we tried to hold on to the faith that we had.

The doctors were fighting to save my daughter's life; not much thought was given to the babies. Time was short. There was no proper nursing staff and no room in the intensive care unit at this hospital, so she had to be transferred to another hospital to prepare for the disaster of aborting the two lives growing in her womb—a decision that seemed right to save her life.

Her chances were slim, and her condition was critical.

Little did I know that God was paving the way with obstacles to delay the surgery.

Realising the seriousness, my faith welled up inside me, and I knew that all who called upon the name of the Lord would be saved. The doctors were grim about her chances of survival.

As I came out of the intensive care unit, I looked at the crowds that had gathered outside, all so concerned, and ready to journey the way with us. Relatives, close friends, everyone concerned, were shattered and feeling despaired.

I knew that if anything could move mountains, it was prayer, and as we got to the other hospital I asked everyone present to go on their knees and pray for Rhonda's life to be saved. At that time, the decision was made to abort the babies so that she would survive.

My faith and trust in God grew stronger at that moment and I knew:
My God would not let me down

As we reached the next hospital, we were called to a meeting with all the doctors. My son Dominic and I went to join them and were told the decision would be ours, to give consent to the termination of the pregnancy, because of the danger to Rhonda. We looked at the six doctors surrounding us, who all said, "Terminate."

Fear, questions, and thoughts tortured me.

How would she deal with the decision that we had made?

Would she understand?

The love she already had for her unborn babies was so intense.

I was caught in a whirlwind of emotions, and deep inside, I wanted to take the chance and not agree to the surgery, but I couldn't. What if we didn't and something terrible happened to her afterwards? Would I be responsible? So, the decision was made to terminate her pregnancy in order to save her life.

In the depth of my heart, I desperately wanted to tell them not to terminate, but my human fears overtook my deep faith. In the meantime, the crowds outside were on their knees, praying and pleading with God to be merciful. God knew, and a moment of divine intervention happened.

Another one of our family doctors, Dr Michael Moses called on a neurologist in Miami and explained the sequence of events. They decided to do an MRI before doing the surgery, because some things in her condition were not adding up.

They believed that her symptoms presented as pre-eclampsia, yet there was still one symptom missing to confirm this diagnosis.

We waited for the results of the MRI; the doctor in Miami later told us that time stood still as he waited, and he felt a divine aura surround him; he felt a deep silence. In the stillness, he heard a voice that said, *"Do not terminate the pregnancy; it's a boy and a girl."*

At that moment, a call came from our neurologist in Florida to discuss the findings of the MRI.

Instantly, the doctor in Miami said, "Her condition is not pre-eclampsia. Do not terminate the pregnancy." This statement took the doctors by surprise, and they were unsure about what they should do. We all sat, stunned in the conference room, with surprised faces.

Meanwhile, her gynaecologist, Dr Agit Kuruvilla, was on his way down to prepare for surgery. The command was given, and we ran downstairs to stop the doctor as he started to prepare to operate on Rhonda. As he was about to enter the operating room, we rushed downstairs and told him to wait.

I believe the heavens opened at that time and wisdom descended on everyone concerned. All this time, the scores of people who had followed us to the hospital were on their knees in the waiting room, praying and pleading for my daughter and her safety.

God had a special plan, and it was about to unfold—a testimony of God's great love and mercy and His sign to us that there is power in prayer when we gather with one heart and mind. He had heard the cries and pleas of everyone to save her life and the lives of the babies. They were destined to live and tell the story of the miracle of their lives.

Thereafter, the doctors continued to stabilise her condition in order to fly her to Miami for medical treatment, in the hope that something could be done to help her present condition.

The preparations were difficult at this time, but again, thanks to another angel that God put in our path, he was able to cross every barrier and locate an air ambulance to fly her out within twenty-four hours. Thank you, Andrew.

The doctors did everything in their medical power to keep Rhonda stable and able to make the flight to the hospital in Miami. I knew that God was leading them and protecting her.

Again, time stood still . . .

Finally, the air ambulance arrived, and Rhonda was transported out of the hospital to meet the aircraft for her flight to Miami. She was then received by the doctor and nurses on board the small aircraft. I wondered, "Would they be able to keep her sedated long enough to reach her destination? Lord, take charge."

Everyone who was gathered outside the hospital looked on with grim faces. What was to happen? Would Rhonda survive the trip? And the babies, would they be affected by her seizures and all the medications? Questions, questions.

Aziz, Rhonda's father, was devastated and heartbroken; he looked so lost and frightened as he watched them transport his beloved daughter into the ambulance for her trip to the aircraft that would take her to Miami.

Rhonda's husband Peter, her brother Dominic, her sister Karlene, and her fiancé Matthew stood by, trying to console Aziz while trying to be brave and hopeful that she would survive the air trip and also that God would continue to take charge and protect her as he had done so far. My son Dominic looked at me and said, with deep emotion, "Mom, if you crumble now, we will all lose hope."

Aziz held on to my dear cousin Lisa and pleaded with her to bring Rhonda back home alive. She was travelling the next morning with my daughter's husband and his family to meet us in hospital in Miami.

It was the most heart wrenching moment for me as I watched the emotions of everyone gathered and tried not to crumble as everyone looked to me for strength and reassurance.

I promised him that all would be well with Rhonda and reminded him our divine Father is a God of mercy and love.

We boarded the aircraft and started our journey to Florida. Only one person was allowed on board with the nurses, and I wanted to be with Rhonda to make sure she felt the presence of a loved one with her. I was only allowed to bring a paper bag with a few belongings, and I learnt at that moment how easy it was to let go of all material things. The following five hours was a nightmare; the aircraft was small and could only hold two medical staff and us.

She had been sedated and intubated with a breathing tube to ensure she did not wake and have further seizures. The air ambulance medical staff was offered extra medication to keep her sedated, and they refused, claiming they had enough. However, as the flight progressed, they began to run out of the medication, and terror seized me as I watched Rhonda coming out of sedation, struggling to reach for the tube in her throat.

I was hunched at the back of the little aircraft, holding onto her feet, trying to balance her body and the stretcher that rocked from side to side as the plane continued its journey.

I prayed in the innermost depth of my heart for God's protection and safety, while pleading with Him to protect the babies from all traumas. It seemed like an eternity before we reached our destination, yet God's grace sustained me. Rhonda was carried in the bosom of our Blessed Mother and the angels who surrounded us.

We finally landed, and she was taken directly to the hospital and into intensive care. We were received in Florida by our family doctor, Dr Joseph Hadeed and our family neurologist, Dr Abe Chamely, who had everything in place for her arrival.

Thank you, Jesus, you never fail me.

There were moments of such fear and uncertainty of what the outcome would be, but my faith grew stronger, as I know that nothing is impossible to God.

"Today '**we walk by Faith, not by sight**' (**2 Corinthians 5:7**). *We perceive Him who is with us. Ours is not a blind trust, it is a proven seeing trust! We walk by faith and have a spiritual vision."21*

Francis Frangipane

"But I have not lost confidence, because I know who it is that I have put my trust in, and I have no doubt at all that He is able to take care of all that I have entrusted to Him, until that day" (2 Timothy 1:12).

Peter remained at her side through it all, and together they began their journey in faith in the darkness of what was to come. After ten days of being hospitalised and having the necessary medical tests done, we were told that her seizures and the terrifying events that had taken place were the result of a brain tumour, which they found on the left frontal side of her brain.

Words cannot explain the thoughts and fears that raced through our minds, because there loomed the possibility that it could be cancerous.

The journey seemed endless and uncertain to us all, and we were called further into the depth of faith, surrendering everything to God, the God I knew would not forsake us.

In the meantime, the doctors planned to get her further into the pregnancy, and she was again put to complete bed rest, until the appointed time for her to deliver her babies. Afterwards, they would then have to make a decision on how to deal with the tumour.

After leaving the hospital, we stayed at my sister's home in Miami; we were fortunate that Joseph, her husband, was a doctor, and it was a great consolation to have him close at hand. God ordained that we would have the love and support of my sister and Joseph around us, to help us through this tumultuous time. Thankfully, our family neurologist also lived close by.

Some days, Rhonda had mini seizures, and we would relive that horrid day when it all began. We took turns staying with her in the room, monitoring her every motion, which was imperative for her well-being and

---

21 Francis Frangipane, http://www.frangipane.org/

that of the babies. There were many sleepless and restless nights for us all, and her discomfort was heartbreaking to witness.

I kept the faith, imploring God to fulfil His promise to her. I knew that God would not bring her this far and allow anything unfortunate to happen to her. Each day, we drew strength from daily readings, one in particular taken from a book that Karlene had given me that Christmas.

Everything seemed to be put into place to help us through that time, yet as each day went by and we reflected on the events, we knew that nothing was in our hands and that we had to surrender to our fears and uncertainty of what the future would bring.

Our time together as a family at my sister's home brought us closer together; we supported each other in our areas of need.

Out of every bad situation, God makes good. Bloom wherever you're planted!

I had no desire to return home, for I knew that my mission was to be with Rhonda, helping and encouraging her through it all. Aziz did not want me to leave her side either, and he visited us from time to time. It's in times like these that we experience the unimportance of all material things, places, and events that we thought were so important.

No one could have imagined her own turmoil, fears, and discomforts. Her nights were so unbearable, yet she endured, for the sake of the two lives within her and the deep desire that she and Peter would one day hold their babies in their arms. We waited patiently, as she visited the doctor's office weekly, until the day came for the delivery of her precious little ones.

Karlene was preparing to get married in March of 2008, and while all of this was happening, we continued to plan her wedding, which was to take place in Miami. It was quite a traumatic time for her as well, because she was filled with so much uncertainty and fear that Rhonda might not make it. She was worried about her health and well-being. She tried to be as joyous as every bride-to-be should, yet trying her best to be faith-filled, trusting that God would continue and complete the miracle that He had started.

I had to share my time, joys, and sorrows, and knew that God would carry me in the palm of His hands, and give me the grace to divide my motherly love between each of my daughters, as the important days of their lives drew near. I drew on the grace and strength of God and believed that He would never give me more than I can handle. He promised that His grace would be sufficient; the only important thing at that time was to continue to witness in faith and glorify Him in my life.

There were times when we thought that Rhonda was ready to deliver the babies, and the fear of her not being able to make her sister's wedding hung over us. The doctors were reluctant to let her go to the wedding, and she was given a choice of either the church or the reception. It was a very emotional time for them both, and the joy of taking part in her only sister's wedding was being taken from them. Finally, she chose to be part of the reception, and we placed our trust in God that He would protect her during the wedding day as we shared in their union on the appointed day.

Again, God showed us that He carried them in the palm of His hand. We all had a wonderful time at the wedding, and a new chapter began in their lives.

Ten days later, Rhonda gave birth to my first grandchildren, whom I almost lost: a beautiful boy and an angelic girl. We were all there to witness this glorious event. It was a double celebration because they were born on my birthday, April 10. My joy was overflowing.

Both sides of parents and siblings gathered together to welcome the little miracles of life that were such precious gifts to us. *To God be the glory, for the great things He has done.*

No god can compare with Him, no miracle to compare with this.

The first stage of this journey had ended, another has begun.

The babies were kept in hospital for a while, to ensure that their health was fine. We did have our fears of any setbacks when Rhonda experienced the seizures. Only time would tell.

Our little baby boy, named Anthony Peter, was kept for ten days in hospital until he was medically cleared. As his parents left the hospital with him in their arms, the joy of holding him surpassed the months of pain and torment.

Our little girl, Elizabeth Ann, had to be kept in the hospital incubator because she was not yet feeding and responding well enough. Our hearts were heavy-burdened as we wondered if all would be well with her. Our prayers continued for her speedy improvement.

One week rolled into weeks, and we watched and waited for signs of more improvement in little Elizabeth. She had to be transported to a specialist children's hospital, and the paediatricians saw there was something more serious with her development and began a series of test to determine her prognosis. The deep joy we experienced at the onset began to decrease as we sensed that our little Elizabeth would face some challenges, and so would we.

God does not give us more than we can handle, and His grace is sufficient for us.

Because my daughter Karlene had been living in Florida, it was even easier for us to stay the six weeks with her after the birth of the babies. I realised then that God had His plan in allowing her to live there, even though we were not in favor at the time.

God shows us that our *thoughts are not His thoughts and all we have to do is trust, trust, trust.*

For three weeks after, we visited her every day in hospital, cradling her and making sure that she felt the love and commitment that we had for her. She had such an angelic look, and already we saw what a special child she would become. She was chosen to glorify God and be a part of His plan to proclaim that our God reigns and that miracles do happen.

Another journey in this healing desert unfolded; we were called again to journey a path with no direction, trusting the signs of the pathway before us. The doctors had their opinions about her prognosis, and we had ours: that one day, God will show His glory. At that point, the doctors were yet to give us a diagnosis of her true condition.

While we were in Miami, my son Dominic had set the date for his wedding: June of 2008. This was to be another joyous occasion, which both Aziz and I have been waiting for many years. He had finally met the girl he wanted to marry, and we had begun wedding plans before this tragic event with Rhonda. Again, I was called to enter into the ups and downs that life can bring, standing on the promises of God that **"the joy of the Lord is my strength" (Nehemiah 8:10).** In the midst of the different seasons of events taking place in my family, I had to be a witness for Jesus and show that He carries us in the palm of His hands when we are heavy laden. I knew that I would be able to do what was necessary for each of my children because **"everyone who calls on the name of the Lord will be saved" (Romans 10:13).**

I made all the necessary arrangements, coordinating the plans for his wedding from the bedside of my daughter. The family's concerns and anxieties of how it would turn out were rising. How would it be possible for me to do what I needed to make this wedding turn out right? I remained steadfast, and with God at my side, I was able to accomplish everything necessary to make this a memorable day for my son and his wife-to-be. I saw where God was doing the planning, and He provided all the help that I need to carry out my plans for the wedding. Thank you, Charmaine, for all the help and support you gave me at this uncertain time.

Because my little granddaughter was kept in hospital for such a long time, fear loomed over us that we would not get home in time for my son's wedding.

I kept the peace and reassured everyone involved that we would make it on time. Ten days before the wedding, we boarded the flight for home. There was such joy in our hearts, and we looked forward with immense hope and joy that all would be well.

The wedding day of my son came, and Rhonda and Karlene were able to share this happy day with their brother, whose joy was complete because we had all come home. People marvelled at what was accomplished in the midst of the tragedies that had taken place in our lives, but as I kept saying, *My God never fails me.*

On my son's wedding day, many blessings were showered upon our family; the celebration was one to remember. The hearts of everyone present were filled with joy as we celebrated together. There was so much to be thankful for: the happiness we felt at the birth of my first grandchildren, the marriage of my daughter, and then the wedding of my son, all within four months. It was accomplished, and the glory of God was seen.

"What lies behind us and what lies before us are only small matters compared to what lies within us."

Author Unknown (possibly Ralph Waldo Emmerson)

St Therese of Lisieux once said:

> *"If I did not simply live from one moment to another, it would be impossible for me to be patient, but I look only at the present. I forget the past and I take good care not to forestall the future. When we yield to discouragement or despair, it is usually because we think too much about the past or the future."*[22]

---

[22] John Beevers, *The Autobiography of St. Therese: The Story of a Soul.* New York: First Image Books Doubleday, 1987

Before returning home, it was evident that my granddaughter would need therapy to develop her feeding skills, so we set about putting things in place for whatever was necessary to improve her development. The journey of faith continued, and we waited for God to reveal His plan for her. It would seem that the entire heavenly courts had commissioned us as a family to be His witness of divine miracles and faith.

The years went by, and we continued to do our part in getting her therapy done, waiting for God's direction while keeping hope and faith.

Rhonda continued to go for her regular check-ups until, after two years of watching and waiting for God's further plan to unfold, she was set for surgery to remove the brain tumour on January 29, 2010.

Preparation was made at the Mayo Clinic in Florida, and the day came for her to again put her life in the hands of God, the Great Physician, and to witness the unfathomable power of her Maker above.

We are not in charge of our life, nor are we masters of our destiny.

The courage and strength she showed was a sign of the graces God had poured out upon her.

The day of surgery began at 3.30 a.m., as we prepared to arrive at the hospital for 5.30 a.m.

The heavens opened, this I knew, for grace carried us to the point when Rhonda was wheeled into surgery. I anointed her with blessed oil and prayed over her before they took her in; I surrendered her to God, who was in charge of that present moment. I even asked the doctors if they would let me anoint and bless their hands, asking God to be their guide. It gave me a sense of peace when they allowed me to do so. Yet, all the unknown anxieties of what could go wrong crowded our minds.

As the world, friends, and family once again prayed for Rhonda's safety, the nine hours of the surgery united us with the fear of "What if?" Peter and I waited for those nine hours locked in prayer, hanging onto our faith that:

"Our God would not let us down."

We were reminded of our Blessed Mother and the disciples who waited in the upper room on the Feast of Pentecost for the outpouring of the Holy Spirit.

Moments of fear and anxiety at the length of time it was taking assailed us, but we kept remembering God's word to us two years ago at the onset of all of this: "Claim this promise today, and look forward to the great things God will reveal to you. Anticipate the fabulously glorious future." These words were part of a daily meditation in a book Karlene had given me for Christmas. It had become our daily words of consolation.

The phone calls kept coming; everyone asked, "Is it over yet?" We had no answer as the hours ticked away, only to trust in God, knowing that He never has, and never will, fail us. I kept on praying, thanking God for what He was about to do for her.

Faith is waiting and hoping, knowing that things unseen and hoped for will blossom with God, the Great Physician and Master of the universe. His care and love for each of His little ones are beyond comprehension.

Finally, the glory of God shone through; the surgeon came out, and we followed him into the lounge to hear the outcome of the surgery. "It could not have gone better," he said. "We've removed 95 percent of the tumour, her speech was not damaged, and we await her recovery." Peter broke down in tears of joy and relief as all the fears and anxieties that were plaguing us were banished.

What a mighty God we serve!

"Thank you, Doctor," I said. "May God continue to bless and guide you. Thank you, thank you."

I saw how God had hand-picked the people He wanted to use for Rhonda's journey of faith and healing, so that she would be able to glorify Him and testify of the wondrous things He had done for her.

Our last uncertainty was waiting for the results of the tumour's biopsy, to determine if she needed any further treatment.

I continued to proclaim that God began a miracle in saving Rhonda's life and that He would complete it. He brought her through the surgery safely, and I knew her results would be fine.

"Jesus, I trust in you."

After about one week, Rhonda was discharged from hospital, and we nursed her until she was able to return home. We felt God's presence carrying us; the moments of her pain and fears at this time, I offered to God for her redemption.

We had to wait for a week for the biopsy results; when the day came, we entered the doctor's office, hoping that the news would be good. Our faith was again tested and we had to trust even deeper, because the doctor had an emergency and could not see us that day. We were being called to trust and wait in blinding faith and hope of the unknown.

"Jesus, I trust in you."

We were told to return later that afternoon. At three o'clock, we sat again in the doctor's office. It was "the hour of mercy," which reminded me of Jesus' crucifixion, and I prayed that God's promise at this hour of mercy would be fulfilled, and that nothing we asked for would be denied us.

We felt like Jesus as he stood before Pontius Pilate, awaiting the sentence. Finally, the doctor came in; still no answer—the biopsy results had not come in as yet, and we were unsure as to what would happen next. We continued three more days of waiting in deeper faith and trust. *Lord, you have heard our every prayer and I know and believe that again you would not fail me.*

We have been pruned and tested in the fire and assured that you purify those you love. We surrendered our every fear and anxiety and bid you take over and continue the work you've started in Rhonda's life. Your desire for her is life in abundance, and you will complete the miracle you started.

"The Lord is my light and my salvation; whom shall I fear?" (Psalm 27:1).

I look forward to the great things you will reveal to us.

All the while, I called upon the Infant Jesus of Prague, whom I always implore during the times of my family illnesses. He has never failed me.

The day came to return home. Still no answer; we left with uncertainty and hope that the call from the doctor would be good news. As we landed in Miami en route to Trinidad, a call came from the doctor. The type of tumour was unknown, but it was not cancerous, and their advice was no treatment, just watch and wait.

Glory and praise to you, oh God. The doctors were baffled, but you showed your power and might. Another miracle to proclaim. They returned home to their children and loved ones, rejoicing and waiting for more to unfold.

Those who put their trust in you would not be forsaken.

I knew you would heal Rhonda and my granddaughter, Elizabeth Ann, and complete the journey of this wondrous story of yet another great miracle.

As I looked upon their twin boy and girl, I realised your love for this family. Rhonda's husband got the boy that he always wanted to carry on the heritage of his family name; this was the only chance. You were born of the line of David and desired that his father's name and genealogy be carried on, just as you did for your Father in Heaven. Thank you for being faithful to your promises.

I pray that the pride and joy that Peter feels when he looks upon his only son, Anthony Peter, would be experienced when Rhonda looks upon her daughter, Elizabeth Ann, believing that one day she will be able to walk and talk.

Later, in August of 2010, at Rhonda's medical check-up, the remnants of her tumour showed a slight increase in growth. This caused concern, and the doctors decided that it would be best to prescribe chemotherapy tablets to her, for between six and twelve months, to ensure no further growth.

This news was unexpected to us, and concern and fears overcame us again. Did this mean that the tumour would become life threatening once more? I refused to believe that this would be so. Were we to become like the disciples who took their eyes off the Lord in the boat at the time of the storm, when they felt their boat sinking? Not so! I remained fixed on the Lord, as He beckoned us to come forward through this clouded journey.

2008

The Desert Time of the Soul

After months of this trying time and what we had to endure in blind faith, I had reached a place of spiritual exhaustion and needed some time away—alone with the Lord. One of my spiritual friends invited me to a retreat in St Lucia. I was reluctant to go, as I thought that I probably should not leave my daughter at that point, but deep within I knew that I needed to go, for myself and the family. I needed to be renewed in the spirit and strength of the Lord, and so I went.

It was a beautiful time away, alone with the Lord and our spiritual director. During one of the sessions, I poured out my heart to the Lord:

My Prayer

Jesus, I thank you for the many wonderful things you have blessed me and my family with.
There is no other God like you: omnipotent and everlastingly gracious.
Take me as your child today and shape the new life you have placed within me.
Your child is weary, yet peaceful. Empower me anew to be the disciple you call me to be—today.
My love for you is an everlasting one, my heart, yours forever.
Stay with me in my time of concern. Quiet the many things that crowd my life today.
I see your hand carrying us safely to the end. When time stood still, when life should have ended, your right hand swooped down and carried us safely to the shores of new life, joy, and happiness.
My gratitude once again, forever now and always, my love beyond all love, my heart all for you.
Thank you, thank you, Papa.

Jesus' Response:

My child, I look with favour upon you, and I see the many efforts you've made. Be at peace and know that I will be your strength and leader. Rest in me as you journey through this time; there is always an end to the road and I await you, along with my heavenly courts, to rejoice with you as you see my glory and power. I love you, my little one.

OCTOBER 21, 2008

With the Lord on Retreat

Meditation on an Object of Nature: The Ixora Plant, which Adorned the Window of the Blessed Sacrament Chapel.

From where did I originate? How did I come into being?

Where was I first planted? What vessel was chosen for me?

What colour was I to be? The choices are many.

Was I placed alongside my siblings—or among others, who are unlike me?

I was natured, watered, fertilised, and pruned, until I became the baby, who was now ready to be uprooted from my safe and secure environment.

Out I came, my destination already chosen for me.

I was looked after, thought about.

Where would I thrive best?

Maybe, I would be carried to be placed among others like myself.

We will complement each other, and be beautiful together, blooming in abundance, that we might feast the eyes of the beloved, and those who look upon us.

Oh! But there are times my little flower falls and my bunch becomes scattered and not so beautiful . . .

Perhaps, it's time for others to be admired, while I wait to bloom again . . .

The sun beats upon me.

The rain drenches my buds, and my buds fall apart.

Yet no other place would I desire to be, but at:

The window of my Beloved.

Mona

JANUARY 15, 2009

Held Captive

Who is man that desires to rob me of my joyous heritage?
A new dawn is upon me, and light opens to sunshine.
The sunshine that belongs to God's beautiful world of creation.
Who is man that draws joy from my being? Alas, he knows not God. For in the midst of sorrow there is joy.
The gladness of being loved by God. Held captive by others' emotions, I struggled to dwell and be nourished by the spirit of God.
If the Lord sets me free, I am free indeed.
I put on the armour of His protection from this world of sadness and gloom. He took on my being that we can be one with Him in suffering. I am God's creation, created to be happy, loved, and free.
I struggle to remain free. Free of man's opinions, emotions, and ideas, resting in my beloved God, who nurtures and guides me towards the horizon of the fullness of life.
A life of radiant sunshine in the darkness. Oh, that I would hold fast to the promises of God . . .
"I have come that you may have life, life in abundance."

Mona

MARCH 21, 2010

Newness (A Message from God)

Behold, I'm doing a new thing. Amidst the trials and tests I have allowed you to endure, you have been victorious through my power working in you. For you are a conqueror, and your trust and faith in me causes me to never fail you. Many cannot understand and will not, for they question too much. Sufficient is it for me that you know the power at work in you.
Keep on plodding; I am with you to the end.

MARCH 22, 2010

Lord, my journey seems so rocky with illnesses and upheavals, but I guess so was yours. Every Lenten season seemed to find me with Aziz journeying through another surgery and the unknown recovery.

I counted his blessings, because when I wonder, again Lord, I think of your journey to Calvary, and count myself lucky that I can partake and be united to your sufferings and those of your Mother.

Obedience to your will brings me peace and allows me to enter into the work you are doing. Thank you, Lord, for choosing me helps me to carry the crosses that I encounter, until your work in me is accomplished.

AUGUST 29, 2010

Lonely Times

Who can climb the mountain of loneliness?
Loneliness that meets us in the form of misunderstanding.
The deep pain of being misjudged, defenceless.
Loneliness that grows deeper and deeper.
When life tends to be ruled by others, not understanding that God is the leader.
The loneliness to remain silent and endure the insults and ridicule, knowing that true humility rests in the silence of no defence.
Who can climb this mountain of loneliness?

Mona

July 11, 2011: Feast of St Benedict

His Love Endures Forever

Every living creature is a reminder of your great love for us and how you provide for all our needs.

As I watch the trust and surrender of your creatures that live on the earth and in the air, how can one doubt that you hold us in the palm of your hands?

No fear or burden should overcome us as we entrust our lives to you.

As I sit and ponder, another miracle has been done; how grateful and privileged I am.

You have brought Aziz out of the depth of darkness and despair in his sickness.

The journey has been rough, and day by day, the boulders pile higher and higher.

Just as you parted the sea and mountain, so too, you continue to clear the way for his life to endure.

The Master has shaped his life once again, through the hands of the doctors.

Thank you, Lord, for hearing the prayers of those who love him;

For giving the doctors the wisdom they need.

For guiding their hands through the procedure.

For sustaining his body through it all.

The sadness, the pain, the anxiety and fear, rolled away, as the doctors came out, confident and secure. They had succeeded again.

One step forward again.

My God Never Fails Me.

"Blessed is the man who meditates on wisdom and who reasons intelligently. He who reflects in his mind on her ways will also ponder her secrets" (Sirach 14:20-21)

CHAPTER 7

The Journey to Calvary

OCTOBER 1, 2011

The Forest Thickens

My journey continued through the healing desert, and when I thought that the forest of uncertainty was clearing, another fear became evident, always apparent in Aziz and his battles to overcome the illness that plagued him.

Oh, how I felt sorry for him, and yet I admired the strength and determination he had to keep fighting, yet weary and sometimes losing faith. I knew that he depended on my strong faith and felt secure that I did the praying for him. He somehow had the confidence and trust that God would hear my prayer for him.

He leaned on me and I on him. I abandoned all, giving up everything, even my love for being in the presence of the Lord at church in the Blessed Sacrament.

I knew that God would be pleased as I turned to my care and nursing of Aziz, like the care of Jesus: **"for I was hungry and you gave me food, I was thirsty and you gave me drink, I was a stranger and you welcomed me, I was naked and you clothed me, I was sick and you visited me, I was in prison and you came to me. Truly, I say to you, as you did it to one of the least of these my brethren, you did it to me"** (Matthew 25:35-36, 40).

Home Again

We returned home once again to continue life in the hope that all would remain well. At the back of our minds and hearts, the fear lingered on: how much longer will his health sustain the bruising and battering of the illness that plagued his life?

All we could do is join together as a family and live life, letting go of all our fears, savouring the good and bad of the uncertainty of his illness.

But it was not long before he was faced with the same challenge of his illness, and we began to realise that what we feared most was upon us. The diseases of cancer and fibrous dysplasia were finally overtaking his body, and we entered into a different fight for survival.

The tumour at the back of his head grew in size, and the pain was becoming unbearable for him.

OCTOBER 4, 2011

Journey of Acceptance

The pain mounted to the heights, and the swelling increased. The disease progressed. Time was crucial.

I prayed for God's promptings and guidance. "When shall I leave to return to the clinic?" The confusion of what was taking place assailed me. The call was mine. "Lord, take charge. Open the way with the doctor's appointments," I prayed.

God's faithfulness always shows the glory of the Great Physician.

We arrived once again at the clinic to face yet another health issue.

This time, my faith was shaken. Somehow I wondered, can I rise above my fears and thoughts?

Is the time drawing near for him to return home to God? And yet I wondered and wondered, "What shall I do, Lord? Show me, give me an answer."

And as always, I prayed. I opened an issue of Magnificat magazine and found this passage:

"God in His providence will use even the apparent evil that attends us in life to some perfecting purpose; out of our littleness, our emptiness, our nothingness God's greatness will flower in an astonishing way. The parables verify that our God is the God who has the care of all—of every situation, every circumstance, every moment. God shows His might precisely when the perfection of [His] power is disbelieved."[23]

"The spirit comes to the aid of our weakness."

We can cave in to our weaknesses out of despair . . . or we can pray with faith.

"Power, whenever you will, attends you."

My physical and spiritual being was slipping away. Like the footsteps in the sands, I felt the Lord and all His beloved ones on earth carrying Aziz and me.

"I am allowed, Lord, to feel that weariness and burden, just as you did in Gethsemane."

---

[23] Todd von Kampen, *Meditations on Scriptures—16th Sunday in Ordinary Time (Year A), 7/16-17/11.* Yonkers, New York: Magnificat magazine, July 16, 2011.

"Into your hands I commend my spirit."

The days ahead were luminous. Aziz's hospitalisation was tiresome, and the ins and outs of his procedures were bleak.

How do I pray this time, Lord? Should I surrender him to you? Deep down I felt his pain and fears of leaving his beloved children, especially his precious little grandchildren, family, and friends.

Finally, the diagnosis came. His fibrous dysplasia, which he's had for forty-five years, had become a cancer of the skull. The bleeding of the skull bone was becoming life threatening. The pain he was experiencing was horrendous. The doctors, as always, were not sure which way to go. What would be less invasive, less life threatening, and would bring some level of comfort to the little time that he had left? I wondered, "Lord, would I experience another miracle in these twenty years of my pleading and interceding for you to save his life?

"Are you really calling him home? Is his work all over?" I tried to believe not.

The doctors tried doing a biopsy to determine if this was another cancer, but he began to bleed profusely and they stopped. This left a wound in the back of his head, and in the months that followed, it became infected and posed a great threat to his life. Each day, this wound had to be cleaned and bandaged; like Mother Teresa, who cleaned the wounds of the sick and poor on the street side, I undertook this with the love and grace of Christ.

I became nurse, comforter, and counselor and endured the cleansing and bandaging of his wound every day. Each day I asked the Lord to bless my hands and bring healing to his wound. There were days that I needed doctors' advice and wondered if I was caring for the area in the right way. I had to put aside my fears and uncertainty and remain strong.

There were times when we had to rush him to hospital because of infection and bleeding; my life at that time became totally devoted to Aziz and being a tower of strength to my family. There was no time to think of myself, and I was confident that God would not abandon me. I knew that He would give me all the grace that I would need to persevere to the end. I refused to have anyone else nurse him, because I knew he was so dependent on my strength and faith.

Just as he had journeyed with me thirty years ago, I now journeyed with him; our love for each other was repaid with care and kindness in our time of need.

November 2011

Surrender

During these last few months of being away from home and in hospital, his children took turns visiting and spending precious moments with him. They too, wondered how much time was left with their dearly beloved father. They hungered to get the most of him and to hear all he had to say to them, yet not wanting to believe that his time was drawing near. Those were the most treasured times spent as a family, and the memories would be added to the lifetime they spent with him, from childhood to adulthood. The sadness in their hearts tried to unite with the sorrow we felt.

We remained away for around six weeks, between the hospital and my daughter's home in the United States. Eventually, I had a strong urge that the time had come for us to return home. The doctors had already told our family that there was nothing they could do for him. I was able to plan our return home with my brother and some friends who had visited the United States on holidays. I needed help to return home.

It was the first time that he did not want to go home, and I believe he knew that his time was drawing near. He was not prepared to accept it yet.

It was through the grace of God that we all managed to return home and spend Christmas with family and friends. I wanted this season of waiting and hope to be a time of joy for our family.

I wanted a time when we could all celebrate together and enjoy those precious moments of life together.

I wondered if this would be the last Christmas we would spend together as a family. As Christmas Day drew near, our two daughters, their spouses, my son and his wife, and our precious six grandchildren surrounded him as much as possible, and we tried to savour the memories we shared together, knowing that his time was short.

It was so painful for us all, because deep down we all knew that this was his last Christmas with us. We celebrated Christmas with joy and sadness and tried to be strong for each other and him, yet preserving his dignity as his illness robbed him of his independence and pride.

We were thankful that we were all together as the New Year began, and we continued to pray for God to spare his life, just a little longer. The support, prayers, and consolation came again from the numerous families and friends who came by to be with us and visit him. This was a great sense of comfort and help.

As he embraced his visitors, I could see the sadness in his eyes as they left; he knew that he might not see them again.

As fate would repeat itself, I received another card from my angel of help when I was ill with my cancer thirty years ago; it read:

"Faith . . . is trusting and believing in a power we can neither see nor touch. It's a feeling born deep within our hearts that keeps us holding even when we feel all our strength is gone."

Author unknown

"Faith is a promise of hope that whispers, 'You'll be okay . . .' even through the darkest times and fills us with power we could never find on our own. It is a bridge between your heart and God."[24]

Jason Blume

On February 14, 2012 (Valentine's Day), Aziz took a turn for the worse; the bleeding in his brain continued. He was rushed to St Clair Hospital, where the neurologists said that he needed immediate surgery in order to arrest the bleeding in his brain. They were, however, very blunt with us and added that he had only a 10 percent chance of surviving the surgery and regaining consciousness. Aziz wanted to take his chances because of his great love for life and his loved ones. The surgery was scheduled, and the surgeons were able to arrest the bleeding in his brain, but as they had suspected, he never regained consciousness after the surgery and slipped into a coma. For twelve days, Aziz was in a coma after his surgery; this was a deeply emotional time for us as a family. We spent our days and nights in the hospital, visiting him in the Intensive Care Unit along with all his other close family members.

We expressed our love, gratitude, and assurance to him that we loved him and appreciated all he had done for us.

---

[24] Faith Magazine High Tea, *Quantum of Faith: A divine gift of Infinite Grace.* Meyersdal Eco Estate Conference Centre, April 21, 2012

We each had our special quiet time alone with him to tell him what was in our hearts and to totally surrender him to God, thus setting him free from all earthly connections.

We were grateful to God for allowing us this sacred time with him, and we were given an opportunity to never suffer regret for not being able to tell him how much he meant to us.

As we watched him suffer, we saw his illness rob him of all dignity and pride, and we had to let go of our selfish love and desire to keep him with us.

My claim to faith was being tested the most at this time, and all my prayers for Aziz moved from physical healing to spiritual healing. The miracle I claimed this time in his illness was victory over darkness and his passing on into the light of Christ that beckoned him to come and feast on the banquet prepared for him.

I had every opportunity to pray deeply at his side and witnessed God's great love for him when He took him back to His heavenly home as His mercy was poured upon him.

On February 26, 2012, Aziz finally gave up the fight, and he was called home to his heavenly Father, who welcomed him into His glorious kingdom, where there is no more pain or suffering. We surrendered him to God, despite the sorrow that we felt, knowing that he would no longer be with us to touch and hold.

Our Trophy

A husband of forty years, determined, stubborn, and strong-willed: qualities that won him his bride and gave him the strength to overcome the challenges of ill-health. He fought life's bitter sweetness.

A husband whose gentle, loving, and caring nature made me love him more and more. He was supportive, even when he disagreed with me.

Peace was his motto. Forty years of no regret, created memories for a lifetime. I love you, Aziz, forever.

A father, who stayed behind and beside his children in battle: in order to open their eyes that they might give names to things, to teach their hands to write and create, and to teach their feet to walk forward.

A father, whose desire was to help his children to truly discover themselves and what was around them. His desire was to make them walk on earth without forgetting the stars.

Their pain hurt him twice as much, and his own pain was suffered half as much in their presence. Their needs surpassed his wants. His love for them overwhelmed and enveloped his life.

A father, who never separated himself from his children. His own life meant something to him, only when he had them all around.

His sons-in-law became his sons.

His daughter-in-law, a shining light.

His precious grandchildren became his lifeline and made his life complete and fulfilled.

They gave him the courage to endure the fight to the very end.

We are blessed.

Thank you, Aziz.

Thank you, Daddy.

Thank you, Uncle.

Thank you, Jido.

May we live always by your example and continue your legacy of **Love and Peace.**

Mona

In loving memory of our beloved Aziz

May 4, 1946-February 26, 2012

MARCH 6, 2012

Life's Purifying Journey

We are called and challenged.
One by one our life unfolds, the dark moments of uncertainties—
We are chosen to journey the winding road.
Joy and sorrow become one,
Our spirits soar as on eagles wings, and we know that all there is to life is
To surrender to the Master's plan.

Mona

"**Blessed is the man who trusts in the Lord, whose trust is the Lord**"
(Jeremiah 17:7).

APRIL 25, 2012: DIVINE MERCY SUNDAY

Dark Night of the Soul

Lord, how I long to retreat to the beautiful sound of the desert, to enter to
the solace of your quieted soul.
The noise of the world around me blocks the serenity of your voice.
I long to write to you the story of my soul and all that's deep within me.
Discipline me that I may set aside that time only for you, that I may enter into
the sacredness of your presence and write my story of your great love for me.
How I feel your presence on this merciful day as I reflect on the love that
pours out of your heart for me and mankind.
Jesus, I trust in you.
I know, Lord, that you are my companion from this day on, and I will
never want for anything, for you are my Father and spouse.
Help me never to doubt, fear, or hide from what the world desires for me,
only Lord:
Bend my heart to your will.
I entrust my life and all my loved ones to the safe embrace of your Sacred
Heart and the gentle heaven of the Immaculate Heart of your Mother.
Alleluia, alleluia, you have risen indeed. Alleluia.

Mona

CHAPTER 8

Revelation on High Places

Sharing the Emmaus Grace

"When the soul does what it can to fulfil its daily obligation and steer its bark as it should, abandoning itself to God, He visits it with His inspirations, at first latent and confused, which if well received, become more and more frequent, more insistent and luminous.

"Then, amidst the joyful and painful events of life, the clash of temperaments, in times of spiritual dryness, amidst the snares of the devil and of men, their suspicions and jealousies, the soul, in its higher regions at any rate, remains always at peace. It enjoys this serenity because it is intimately persuaded that God is guiding it; in abandoning itself to Him, it seeks only to do His will and nothing more. Thus, it sees Him everywhere under every external guise and makes use of everything to further its union with Him. Sin, by its very contrast, will recall the infinite majesty of God.

"The soul has less need of reasoning and methods in its prayer and meditation, or for its guidance; it has become more simplified in its mode of thought and desire. It follows, rather, the interior action of God in its soul, which makes itself felt not so much by the impressions of ideas, as though the instinct or the necessity imposed by circumstances, where only one course is possible. It perceives at once the depth of meaning in some phrase in the Gospels which has not previously impressed it. God gives it an understanding of the scriptures, as He gave to the two disciples on the way to Emmaus. The simplest sermons are a source of enlightenment, and it discovers treasures in them; for God makes use of these as a means that He himself may enlighten the soul, just as a great artist may use the most ordinary implement, the cheapest pencil, to render a great masterpiece, a wonderful picture of Christ or the blessed virgin.

"In God's dealings with souls who abandon themselves to Him, much remains obscure, mysterious, disconcerting, and impenetrable, but He makes it all contribute to their spiritual welfare, and someday, they will see that what was, at times, a cause of profound desolation to them was the source of much joy to the angels."[25]

Father Reginald Garrigou-Lagrange

---

[25] Father Reginald Garrigou-Lagrange, *Sharing the Emmaus Grace*. Yonkers, New York: Magnificat magazine, April 2012

Prayer of Abandonment

"Father,
I abandon myself into your hands;
do with me what you will.
Whatever you may do, I thank you:
I am ready for all, I accept all.

Let only your will be done in me,
and in all your creatures—
I wish no more than this, O Lord.

Into your hands I commend my soul:
I offer it to you with all the love of my heart,
for I love you, Lord, and so need to give myself,
to surrender myself into your hands without reserve,
and with boundless confidence,
for you are my Father."[26]

Charles de Foucauld
The Desert Father

---

[26] Charles De Foucauld, Robert Ellsberg, *Charles De Foucauld: Writings*. Maryknoll, NY: Orbis Books, 1999

MAY 8, 2012

Lasting Memories

Memories keep flooding in as I think of my late husband, Aziz, in his life and passing. If I dare to summarise his life and how he lived, I would remember his drive for life in every area and stage of it.

The greatness of a man is not known, until he's great no more.

Aziz Hadeed was a great man, who came to Trinidad from his hometown, Amar al-Hosn, in Syria. I can remember the enthusiastic young boy he was at age twenty-one.

Coming to join his brothers in business and to make a better life for himself and his future, he forged forward to learn the language, make himself a part of the community, and understand the culture of the country he chose to live in.

At the time, I was sixteen years old and still in school; we met at family gatherings and were just friends. As time went on, he started to show a deeper interest in our friendship. Given that I was still quite young and in school, my mother was not very encouraging. We endured two years of a rocky courtship, trying to get to know each other with intense resistance from my mother. It was during this time that I realised how much he really loved me. He often told me how he could not live without me and would do anything to make me his wife.

I remembered the times I felt that, just maybe, I should end the relationship because it was causing too much pain and hurt in the family. He even told me that he would elope with me if my mother did not give consent, and this made me smile to think that he would go to such lengths to have me as his wife.

I found myself praying harder and fervently each day for God to guide me to make the right decision; if it was His will, I would have the strength to endure the fight. My mother was never in full approval, because from her point of view, she was protecting her young daughter.

On June 20, 1971, Aziz and I got married, and there began our journey of bittersweet memories of happiness and sadness, surrounding a life of having a family and battling the ravages of the illnesses that plagued him.

This was when I first witnessed the trait of determination in him. The fortitude that he possessed became the lifeline on which he hung, as he beat the odds of the illnesses that he had to endure for twenty years.

As a father, his love for his son and two daughters was something I often marvelled at; he would always deprive himself in all ways to ensure that they would want for nothing. At times, however, his bleeding heart of love for them over-powered his reasoning.

Like all fathers who desired the same for their children, he was like our divine Father. There was an intensity in how he loved, and I was able to experience this in our relationship as husband and wife.

All of his extended family and friends witnessed his essence. No one ever became his enemy, and he would do everything in his power to help when needed. He was so loved that he could say anything to anyone, and they would not be hurt. His sense of humour remained with him to the end, even in his pain and sorrow.

In spite of the endless types of cancers and other ailments that he experienced, some so painful and crippling, he never gave up the fight to overcome and continue being a father, husband, or friend, and an example of strength and resilience.

He would live life each day as if he had no pain or fears of what may come out of his illnesses and showed that where there's life, there's hope.

The last six months of his life were stamped in my heart and mind; I often reflect on those three stages before he drew near to the end. Finally, when he could no longer endure the fight against his illnesses, he gracefully gave up and left us. The memories would fill a lifetime, and the examples would be hard to follow, but the fortitude that carried him is our driving force, as we too journey through life.

As I ponder and reflect on the last two months, I understood his pensive moments and urgency to ensure that all was well with his loved ones and that they would never be in want.

I remained at his side and nursed him through those times when he felt all dignity had left him. I tried to give him the courage he needed when his own fears overcame him, and I hid my own fears and tiredness, just to ensure that his strength to fight would not fail him.

When we finally returned home from the hospital, on January 30, 2012, little did we all know that in two weeks, he would succumb to a brain bleed and slip into a coma. We agreed to surgery, knowing that he would have wanted to take the chance. He survived the surgery but never came out of the coma. For twelve days he fought the fight, until finally he went home to his eternal Father, who was waiting for him.

My love for him grew even deeper as I remembered all the past incidents and occasions when the kindness of his heart overwhelmed me. The care that he showed for the people he knew was always a wonder to me.

Now that he's gone, I miss his presence and his very being that filled my heart and our surroundings. His simplicity, humility, and profound love for me, his kids, and grandchildren will never be forgotten. His gentle spirit and love for life would be imprinted in our hearts and locked away, where the pains we endure cannot touch it.

Farewell, my beloved, you will be missed, and our days of courtship and the fight to belong to each other will be engraved in my heart and continue to give me the strength to carry on. Our children will reflect the love we shared; they were shown what a great father and grandfather you were. How precious you were to us, and our sadness lies in knowing that we can't hug and kiss you again and tell you how much we love you and appreciate what you have done for us.

Rest in the arms of Jesus and suffer no more, for you have won the crown of glory that you rightfully deserve.

I realised that I now had to take up the role of father and mother, and fill the void that was left in his passing. My children, especially my son-in-law, who had worked with him, would miss him sorely; they looked to me for consolation and hoped that they could survive his passing and still be joyous. My son had lost his father, who was at his side throughout his life, guiding and supporting him; he now had to stand on his own, remembering the times he consoled him just by saying, "Don't worry, son, everything will work out."

I had to now assure him that I would be at his side to give him whatever help I could, whenever he needed it. My daughters had lost one of the greatest fathers, who loved them beyond everything in this world, and they would miss his loving embrace and comfort. His presence had a way of consoling them, no matter what, and his gentle spirit would always be remembered.

His grandchildren knew him for only a short while, and we pledged to never allow them to forget him. I promised myself to do the best I could to fill the void in their hearts and mind.

God never gives us more than we can handle.

Mona

May his soul and the souls of all the faithful departed through the mercy of God rest in peace. Amen.

SEPTEMBER 27, 2012

The Desolation of Connection

Lord, when life and relationships disappoint you, the soul feels separated from those around.

I come to the reality that no matter what, you alone, Lord, are constant and abiding.

Your love for me will always be a blanket of comfort that keeps me safe.

I'm locked in the realm of your warmth and security, knowing that no harm can come to me, no loneliness too great to bear.

Your heavenly court makes music in my silence, and the joy of the sounds of the heavenly court fills my being and lifts me high.

You call me apart to hear your voice alone and block the clamour and noise of this empty world.

Oh, would the sweetness of your melody overcome the emptiness—then the soul is restored to its divine state.

Mona

St Francis de Sales once said:

"God leaves you in this state for his glory and your own great profit; He wants your poverty to be the throne of His mercy, and your helplessness the seat of His omnipotence."[27]

---

[27] E. Stopp, *St. Francis de Sales: Selected Letters.* 1st ed. London: Faber & Faber, 1960

MAY 4, 2013

Pilgrimage to France, Spain, and Portugal

It had been almost three years since my last pilgrimage, and I yearned to be united with my Lord in serenity and to surrender after the death of Aziz. I was happy that I could go and looked forward to seeing how our Blessed Mother would lead me into the heart of Jesus, her Son.

This was to be my quiet time with the Lord, listening to His voice and understanding the true message of His new call to me from here on.

A new journey had begun.

The message of our spiritual director was as follows:

Make space in your heart to receive the graces that God and His Blessed Mother desire to give you on this pilgrimage, to be who you were created to be and who you really are.

I returned once again to make a journey of faith, to witness the miracles of your Blessed Mother, who you have chosen to draw me closer to the union of the two hearts.

It's all coming together again, Lord: the union of Hearts, that of your Mother, and yours as we sit in adoration before you and remember her commission to us when she said, **"Do whatever He tells you"** (John 2:5). The only request Jesus ever made to His apostles: **"Could you not watch with Me one hour?"** (Matthew 26:40).

There were so many thoughts in my head and heart, and I needed to know if this was His will for me or my own will and desires. There were three things in particular that I needed His guidance with, and throughout the trip, I waited for Him to unfold His plan.

As we travelled to the sacred shrines, there was a message for me; God showed me my weaknesses and pride. I felt He was calling me to forgive all those who have forgiven me, with a sincere spirit of atonement and reconciliation. I asked Him for the grace to truly forgive and put the past behind me. I experienced the mercy of God and saw the rewards and blessings that He showered upon me as I abandoned all my hurts and pains to Him.

At the Grotto of our Blessed Mother at Lourdes, I sat in silence over the river, facing the spot where our lady appeared and gazed in reverence upon her face. I could hear her speak, heart to heart, and Jesus drawing me closer in.

"Lord, reveal to me what you are saying to me through your Blessed Mother. I love you."

We completed our visits to the chosen shrines, and the message of each came together for my life. I was able to discern the path my life should take and what the Lord was preparing for me.

I had been walking the pilgrim's way for thirty years; the story of St James, which I had opened at the time of my illness, blossomed into the truth of my life. I was finally able to put the story of my illness and healing into the meaning of the passage I found in **James 1:2: "Count it all joy, my brethren, when you meet various trials."**

I shared with the group the journey of my sufferings and how I endured the many things that came my way.

Jesus is our rock, and we stand on the pillar of faith, which is the foundation of Jesus through His mother and father.

Many people choose to imitate the way of St James by travelling from one state to another on foot, experiencing the hardships, yet encountering the encouragement and offer of food, drink, and a place to rest until they reach the Church of St James in Compo Stella, Spain.

The hospitality they shared with them was an example of how we should live in this world with each other and a reminder that as Jesus journeyed to Calvary, He too had the good Samaritan, who was there to help him on.

It was symbolic of our call to be Christ-like, to feed the hungry, to clothe the naked, and to give drink to the thirsty. They knew to complete this journey meant hardships, sacrifice, patience, endurance, and most of all, joy: a reminder of what we also experience on our life's journey. It was a purifying and humbling time because of the inconvenience they were called to endure, but they kept steadfast in overcoming the obstacles and exhaustion that could have easily caused them to give up.

Many of us are tempted on our journey to give up, but through the grace of God and our love for Him, we continue and endure to the end. I felt that I had made the spiritual journey with St James, and I delighted in my sufferings and the glory of what came my way afterwards.

I hope, as you reach the end of my faith journey, you understand why I chose this name for my book; *The Healing Desert in the Sands of Time* carried me through the trials of my call. I learnt also to depend on only

God's voice leading me and not the voices of the world, whose call may have been different. It's hard at times, because not everyone shares your spirituality and relationship with the Lord.

I would like to leave you with a reading that I came upon, and I pray that you might find solace in your own journey, remembering that God created you in His image and likeness. Remember too, that we all have our own purpose and mission on this earth, if only we learn *how* to listen to His voice and say, "Yes Lord, here I am."

Be Yourself

"We are the most appealing to our friends, and the happiness, when we were completely ourselves. But it is a constant struggle because, as scripture teaches, the world is always trying to press us into its mould.
The mould of the world is the mould synthetic,
The mould of the artificial, the mould of the celluloid, the 'Plastic Person.'
The world cries, 'You've got to be young and you've got to be tanned. You've got to be thin and you've got to be rich. You've got to be great.'

"But scripture says, 'You don't have to be any of those things. You simply have to be yourself, at any age, as God made you, available to Him so that He can work in and through you to bring about His Kingdom and Glory.' Now relax. Trust Him and be yourself!"[28]

Luci Swindoll

A Step Beyond

The road lies before you
Life is open to you
The direction can be clear if only you mark it well; there will be twists and turns that narrow and widen.
That's Life's Road
To every turn there is a sign post.
Search well for it; follow the ways of God not man
For all roads lead to home. The place ordained for you by God alone.
Seek his wisdom, guidance, and way, and you will surely reach your final destination: Chosen for You Alone.

Mona

---

[28] Luci Swindoll, *You Bring the Confetti, God Brings the Joy*. Nashville: Thomas Nelson, 1997

CHAPTER 9

Conclusion

My Gift to God

As I come to the end of my faith journey of *The Healing Desert in the Sands of Time*, I wish to share with all of my readers that the journey to the completion of this book has not been easy. The obstacles that came my way were numerous, and I was tempted to give it up, but I knew that when we desire to glorify God in our lives, and give Him the praise for the great things He has done for us, the road becomes rocky with trials and joy.

The desire to make known the greatest of our Father in Heaven comes with a responsibility, but just as I proclaimed that nothing was too great for my God to do for me, so too, writing this book was not too much for me, in spite of the setbacks and interruptions. Many thoughts tormented me about why I should write this book, but I had to keep my heart fixed on the Lord and block out my human thoughts.

All through the time of writing, I had to put into practice the faith I proclaimed throughout this book, from deciding to compose it, to choosing my editor, to deciding on the right publisher, and to dying to self and asking for the help that I needed.

I could not have completed this book without the prayer support of those I chose to carry me in prayer: Well done, good and faithful stewards; united, we can do what God calls us to. Thank you.

If inspired pen is put to paper, with much fear and uncertainty, it becomes a reality.

It's Not Over

I know that as my faith journey continues, new chapters in my life will open up, and as I continue to call on the Almighty to sustain me for the work He still has for me, I see His hand leading me where many would not go or would fear to walk.

My grandchild Elizabeth Anne (whom we named after St Elizabeth Anne Seaton) has been the inspiration and guidance to God's next call to me.

She is physically challenged and not able to explore the services necessary to help her attain the best of her abilities, only because of the lack of a complete special needs clinic in our country.

I know that one day, God will heal her, and she will be a witness of His glory, as my daughter Rhonda and I have been and we will continue to proclaim what miracles the Lord has worked among us:

> *Some may never walk,*
> *They may never talk,*
> *Be self-sufficient or tell their story,*
> *Our hearts cry out for help on their behalf.*
> *Parents have nowhere to turn, they live in turmoil, their energies wasted, their hearts are heavy laden.*
> *We can make a difference.*

God calls me to make a difference, and in faith I step out to fulfill the call He now makes to me.

In receiving the approval of this book from the publishers, I suddenly felt warmth in my heart and the financial challenge before me of being able to make this dream become a reality.

All proceeds from my book will be put toward the building of this special needs clinic; I ask my readers to pray that the doors and windows to this pathway will be opened, and the power of the Holy Spirit will blow in.

The journey continues.

God bless you all.

Mona

Bibliography

1. Henri J. M. Nouwen, *The Inner Voice of Love*. New York: First Image Books Doubleday, 1998.
2. Carlo Carretto, *The Desert and Beyond* (a compilation of three books: *Letters from the Desert, In Search of the Beyond,* and *Love Is for the Living*). London: Darton, Longman & Todd, 1987.
3. Carlo Carretto, *Letters from the Desert Father.* 2nd ed. Maryknoll, NY: Orbis Books, 1990.
4. Carlo Carretto, *Why Oh Lord? The Inner Meaning of Suffering.* Maryknoll, NY: Orbis Books, 1986.
5. Ruth Burrows, *Interior Castle Explored: St. Teresa's Teaching on the Life of Deep Union with God.* New York: Paulist Press, 2007.
6. Thomas Merton, *The Seven Storey Mountain.* Orlando, FL: Harcourt Brace, 1999.
7. Thomas Merton, *Soul Searching.* Collegeville, MN: Liturgical Press, 2008.
8. Brian Kolodejchuk, *Come Be My Light: Mother Teresa.* New York: Doubleday Religious Publishing Group, 2007.
9. Mother Teresa, *Where There Is Love, There Is God: A Path to Closer Union with God and Greater Love for Others.* New York: Doubleday Religious Publishing Group, 2010.
10. Ana Ganza, *A Journey of Hope—Authorized by Mother Teresa.* Angel Publishing, 2012.
11. Christian D. Larson, *Your Forces and how to Use Them.* 1st ed. Chicago: The Progress Co. 1912.
12. Mother Teresa, *Jesus Is My All in All: Praying with the Saint of Calcutta.* New York: Doubleday, 2008.
13. Mother Teresa, *The Joy in Loving: A Guide to Daily Living.* New York: Penguin Compass, 2000.
14. Henri J. M. Nouwen, *Here and Now: Living in the Spirit.* New York: Crossroad Publishing Company, 1994.
15. Glyn Evans, *God's Perfect Plan for Us.*
16. Henri J. M. Nouwen, *The Wounded Healer: Ministry in Contemporary Society.* London: Darton, Longman & Todd, 1994.

17. John Beevers, *The Autobiography of St. Therese: The Story of a Soul*. New York: First Image Books Doubleday, 1987.
18. Thomas Merton, *I Have Seen What I Was Looking For*. Hyde Park: New City Press, 2005.
19. Theo H. Zweerman, Edith van den Goorbergh, *Saint Francis of Assisi: A Guide for Our Times*. Leuven, Belgium: Peeters, 2007
20. Anne Morrow Lindbergh, *Gift from the Sea*. New York: Pantheon, 1991
21. Martin Buber, *I and Thou*. Eastford, CT: Martino Fine Books, 2010
22. Marie Shropshire, *In Touch with God: How God Speaks to a Prayerful Heart*. Eugene, OR: Harvest House Publishers, 2005.
23. Theodore Roethke, *The Waking: Poems 1933-1953*. New York: Doubleday, 1953.
24. Jonathan Edwards, *A Treatise Concerning Religious Affections*. New York: Cosimo Classics, 2007.
25. Sara Teasdale, *Love Songs*. Charleston, SC: Forgotten Books, 2012
26. Lao Tzu, *Tao Te Ching*. 1st ed. Boston, MA: Shambhala, 2007
27. Francis Frangipane, http://www.frangipane.org/
28. Kahlil Gibran, *The Prophet*. Hertfordshire: Wordsworth Editions, 1997.
29. Helen Steiner Rice, *Loving promises: especially for you*. Grand Rapids, Mchigan: F. H. Revell Co., 1975.
30. Todd von Kampen, Meditations on Scriptures—16th Sunday in Ordinary Time (Year A), 7/16-17/11. Yonkers, New York: Magnificat magazine, July 16, 2011.
31. Faith Magazine High Tea, *Quantum of Faith: A divine gift of Infinite Grace*. Meyersdal Eco Estate Conference Centre, April 21, 2012.
32. Father Reginald Garrigou-Lagrange, *Sharing the Emmaus Grace*. Yonkers, New York: Magnificat magazine, April 2012.
33. Charles De Foucauld, Robert Ellsberg, *Charles De Foucauld: Writings*. Maryknoll, NY: Orbis Books, 1999.
34. E. Stopp, *St. Francis de Sales: Selected Letters*. 1st ed. London: Faber & Faber, 1960.
35. Luci Swindoll, *You Bring the Confetti, God Brings the Joy*. Nashville: Thomas Nelson, 1997.

About the Author

Mona Hadeed is an active member of the parish of St Finbar's Roman Catholic Church, as well as a devoted mother of three children and grandmother of six. Born and raised in the Caribbean island of Trinidad, she was instrumental in the start of Eucharistic Adoration in her community in 1996. In 2013 she was part of a committee that spearheaded the building of a new Perpetual Adoration chapel in her parish of St Finbar's.

For over twenty-five years, she was the leader of the Holy Family Prayer Group, which is still active today. She is an avid writer who has answered God's call to spread His message of faith and love.

She has been on numerous pilgrimages to the Holy Land, as well as to the many Marian shrines around the world such as Fatima, Lourdes, Medjugorje, and Betania. From these pilgrimages, she has gained much spiritual insight and healing, in addition to strengthening her faith for her life's journey.

---

[29]   Gary Jordan Photography